D0776269

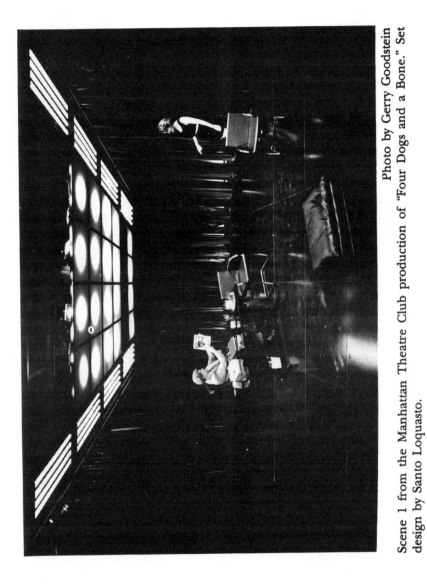

Photo by Gerry Goodstein

Scene 1 from the Manhattan Theatre Club production of "Four Dogs and a Bone." Set design by Santo Loquasto.

FOUR DOGS AND A BONE

and

THE WILD GOOSE

BY JOHN PATRICK SHANLEY

★

★

DRAMATISTS
PLAY SERVICE
INC.

FOUR DOGS AND A BONE and THE WILD GOOSE
Copyright © 1995, Patrick Shanley

All Rights Reserved

CAUTION: Professionals and amateurs are hereby warned that performance of FOUR DOGS AND A BONE and/or THE WILD GOOSE is subject to payment of a royalty. The Plays are fully protected under the copyright laws of the United States of America, and of all countries covered by the International Copyright Union (including the Dominion of Canada and the rest of the British Commonwealth), and of all countries covered by the Pan-American Copyright Convention, the Universal Copyright Convention, the Berne Convention, and of all countries with which the United States has reciprocal copyright relations. All rights, including without limitation professional/amateur stage rights, motion picture, recitation, lecturing, public reading, radio broadcasting, television, video or sound recording, all other forms of mechanical, electronic and digital reproduction, transmission and distribution, such as CD, DVD, the Internet, private and file-sharing networks, information storage and retrieval systems, photocopying, and the rights of translation into foreign languages are strictly reserved. Particular emphasis is placed upon the matter of readings, permission for which must be secured from the Author's agent in writing.

The English language stock and amateur stage performance rights in the United States, its territories, possessions and Canada for FOUR DOGS AND A BONE and THE WILD GOOSE are controlled exclusively by DRAMATISTS PLAY SERVICE, INC., 440 Park Avenue South, New York, NY 10016. No professional or nonprofessional performance of either of the Plays may be given without obtaining in advance the written permission of DRAMATISTS PLAY SERVICE, INC., and paying the requisite fee.

Inquiries concerning all other rights should be addressed to Creative Artists Agency, 162 Fifth Avenue, 6th Floor, New York, NY 10010. Attn: George Lane.

SPECIAL NOTE

Anyone receiving permission to produce FOUR DOGS AND A BONE and/or THE WILD GOOSE is required to give credit to the Author as sole and exclusive Author of the Play(s) on the title page of all programs distributed in connection with performances of the Play(s) and in all instances in which the title(s) of the Play(s) appears for purposes of advertising, publicizing or otherwise exploiting the Play(s) and/or a production thereof. The name of the Author must appear on a separate line, in which no other name appears, immediately beneath the title(s) and in size of type equal to 50% of the size of the largest, most prominent letter used for the title(s) of the Play(s). No person, firm or entity may receive credit larger or more prominent than that accorded the Author. The following acknowledgment must appear on the title page in all programs distributed in connection with performances of the Play(s):

FOUR DOGS AND A BONE was originally produced
by the Manhattan Theatre Club on October 12, 1993.

Table of Contents

FOUR DOGS
AND A BONE

Quotes from the Ancients on the Film Business

"Savage is he who saves himself."
—Leonardo Da Vinci

"Among other evils which being unarmed brings you,
it causes you to be despised."
—Machiavelli

"Victory shifts from man to man."
—*The Illiad,* Homer

"He has not acquired a fortune;
the fortune has acquired him."
—Bion, 300 B.C. or so

"I would rather be wrong with Plato,
than right with such men as these."
—Cicero, 100 B.C. or thereabouts

"I love treason but hate the traitor."
—Julius Caesar

"O accurst craving for gold!"
—Virgil

"Quo Vadis?" (Where are you going?)
—Said to Jesus on his way to the cross

"The Medici created and destroyed me."
—Leonardo Da Vinci

FOUR DOGS AND A BONE was produced by Manhattan Theatre Club (Lynne Meadow, Artistic Director; Barry Grove, Managing Director), in New York City, in October, 1993. It was directed by John Patrick Shanley; the set design was by Santo Loquasto; the costume design was by Elsa Ward; the lighting design was by Brian Nason; the sound design was by Bruce Ellman and the production stage manager was Donna A. Drake. The cast was as follows:

BRENDA .... Mary-Louise Parker
BRADLEY.. Tony Roberts
COLLETTE.. Polly Draper
VICTOR .... Loren Dean

FOUR DOGS
AND A BONE

ACT ONE

Scene 1

An office. Chairs.

BRENDA.   My brother's baby-sitter used to have sex with him. Think about it. I know that's like a guy's ultimate fantasy. A young guy anyway, but it really messed him up. He lives in a Jeep. I've been incested. By my brother, my father and my sister. It's a chain. My father doesn't show his feelings. He's a genius doctor but he's so like dead. I took care of him for a while when he left my mother. We kept house. That was the happiest time in my life. When my father got married again, I started this primal wailing, jilted crying thing. Everybody was embarrassed. It was so obvious. I ended up on the street. I was a junkie.

BRADLEY.   What about your other brother?

BRENDA.   You know about him?

BRADLEY.   Yeah.

BRENDA.   He's my step-brother.

BRADLEY.   Oh.

BRENDA.   I don't want anything from him, Bradley.

BRADLEY.   But didn't he do anything when you fell on hard times?

BRENDA.   Yeah. He's why I left L.A. My identity was in danger.

BRADLEY.   Identity. *(He takes out a magazine and shows her the cover. Steven Spielberg is on the cover.)* Do you know who this is?

9

BRENDA.   Steven Spielberg?

BRADLEY.   Wrong. This is me with 500 million dollars and a beard.

BRENDA.   I don't understand.

BRADLEY.   Sometimes character is an obstacle to be overcome. How do you like your job?

BRENDA.   I love it. It's a great part. I chanted for it.

BRADLEY.   Oh, that's right, you're a ... Buddhist?

BRENDA.   Chanter. I'm a chanter. I chant for things I want.

BRADLEY.   What's the chant?

BRENDA.   I hope you don't mind, Bradley. I can't tell you.

BRADLEY.   Oh. Okay.

BRENDA.   It's just some words.

BRADLEY.   That's okay.

BRENDA.   You say them over and over.

BRADLEY.   Uh-huh.

BRENDA.   If it wasn't for these words, I'd be in an insane asylum today. Like my mother. My mother made a house out of like a box and lived outdoors. She wouldn't come in. Outta the winter snow she forbore to come in. She was insane. I wish she'd chanted. I wish I could go back in time and give her the chant.

BRADLEY.   I wish you could, too. So you're seeing Victor.

BRENDA.   How'd you know?

BRADLEY.   It's obvious. The way you look at him.

BRENDA.   I chanted for him.

BRADLEY.   What do you mean?

BRENDA.   I chanted. That's how I got him.

BRADLEY.   He likes you, too.

BRENDA.   You think so? How can you tell?

BRADLEY.   He wrote a new scene for you in the movie. He's building up your part.

BRENDA.   That has nothing to do with anything.

BRADLEY.   The director thinks it does.

BRENDA.   George thinks that.... What?

BRADLEY.   It's all right. It's natural. It may even be good for the picture.

BRENDA.   What?

BRADLEY.   I thought you'd end up with George, not Victor, but what do I know?

BRENDA.   Every movie has like one central person behind it. Sometimes it's the director. Sometimes it's the writer.

BRADLEY.   Sometimes it's the producer.

BRENDA.   I didn't mean to leave you out.

BRADLEY.   Bear with me, Brenda, but everyone knows you're the one on this film that's going somewhere.

BRENDA.   Really? I'm just happy to be included with so many talented people.

BRADLEY.   Bear with me, Brenda, but Victor got lucky. This script *could* be a good movie, but if George hadn't picked it up and decided, you know, I'm doing this! — Victor would be back Off-Off Broadway, where maybe he belongs.

BRENDA.   I think this script is so wonderful. Most scripts ...

BRADLEY.   Bear with me, Brenda.

BRENDA.   Sorry.

BRADLEY.   This is an eight million dollar movie we're shooting for five. It's my job to make those numbers work, they don't work, so I'm under a little pressure right now. Maybe that's what makes me indiscreet, but you're the star of this movie, Brenda. Not the director, not the writer, not me. And certainly not Collette.

BRENDA.   You don't think she's good?

BRADLEY.   She's a stage actress. This is a film.

BRENDA.   But she seems really good to me.

BRADLEY.   She's a stage actress.

BRENDA.   You mean she's too big?

BRADLEY.   Way too big. She makes these faces that are supposed to be, I don't know, cute. It's grotesque. It's Kabuki. I'll tell you this. Her closeups are getting the wrong kind of laughs in dailies.

BRENDA.   Oh no.

BRADLEY.   Your stuff's sensational.

BRENDA.   I haven't done anything yet. Except the staircase.

BRADLEY.   There's a shot, you look up to answer him, I leaned over to George. I said, She's a star.

BRENDA.   What did he say?

BRADLEY.   He nodded. Anyway, he moved his head. I mean, he may have been agreeing with me.

BRENDA.   I find it hard to know what he's thinking.

BRADLEY.   He's weak.

BRENDA.   Collette seems so skilled to me.

BRADLEY.   I know this is going to sound cold, but she's just a stiff. Her eyes are dead.

BRENDA.   What does Peter think?

BRADLEY.   Peter? All Peter cares about is the light. He's a cameraman, he's a gadget geek. He's not interested in human beings. You know that light meter he keeps holding up to your face?

BRENDA.   Oh, is that what that is?

BRADLEY.   What did you think it was?

BRENDA.   A makeup analyzer?

BRADLEY.   Never mind. That's all Peter cares about. The reading on that meter. If he tells you, after a take, that that was really good, that means he liked the exposure. He's not interested in acting, in story. He's not even interested in money. He is an idiot I hope savant. George, on the other opposite hand, is a golden boy. Acres of brains, connections for days, more charms than Salome. A cunning fuck. But weak. And weak is death in a director.

BRENDA.   So you're telling me the movie's no good?

BRADLEY.   No, that's not what I'm telling you, Brenda. I'm telling you that I've been in dailies, and we had an idea of what this movie's supposed to be, but now the movie's talking back to us. The movie is telling US what it is. And if we ignore that, if we ignore what the movie's telling us to our faces, then we've blown it. Then the movie's no good. Then it's a bad movie.

BRENDA.   So what's the movie saying?

BRADLEY.   The movie is saying that YOU, not Collette, is the star of the movie. The movie is saying that it's tired, that it's too long, that it wants to get rid of about SEVEN SCENES. The movie is saying that the director is weak so we've got to be strong!

BRENDA.   Who?

BRADLEY. You and me! And by default, or through you, somehow, Victor!

BRENDA. What about Victor?

BRADLEY. You seem to have some influence with him! He wrote a scene for you!

BRENDA. It was his idea!

BRADLEY. Brenda, the point is we can save this movie!

BRENDA. Look, I don't know.

BRADLEY. The director is weak!

BRENDA. I don't know how to judge a director, Bradley. This is my first movie.

BRADLEY. The director should be strong! Very strong!

BRENDA. Well, I guess that's true.

BRADLEY. He should tell the writer, LOOK, it's too long! We don't have the money! You've got to cut *seven scenes!*

BRENDA. What scenes?

BRADLEY. None of your scenes! Collette's scenes!

BRENDA. But she's the star! Everybody thinks she's great! She'd be so upset!

BRADLEY. We've got to cut her out of the picture!

BRENDA. Cut her out? But she's the star of the picture!

BRADLEY. You're the star!

BRENDA. But what about the story?

BRADLEY. The ending's too pat. It should be more mysterious. If we cut out Collette, it'll leave a mystery there where she was.

BRENDA. That's true.

BRADLEY. But that's a good point that you're making. We would need more money.

BRENDA. Money? I didn't make the point ...

BRADLEY. We'd need some bridge scenes to span the Collette gaps. So Dustin Murphy's your brother?

BRENDA. I don't like people to know that.

BRADLEY. No? It's what got you the job on this picture.

BRENDA. That's not true!

BRADLEY. It was down to you and another girl. Your brother's somebody famous. A little of that sparkle rubbed off on you and made you just a little more attractive to George.

BRENDA. I chanted to get this job.

BRADLEY. I'm sure the other girl chanted, too. But her brother wasn't a movie star.

BRENDA. He's not my brother, he's my step-brother.

BRADLEY. If he heard you were on the verge of breaking through in the business, on the verge of becoming a major second earner on his family tree, wouldn't he help you?

BRENDA. What kind of help?

BRADLEY. Money, jing-jing, money.

BRENDA. You know a lot of people have tried to take advantage of my connection to Dustin, but you've gotta be the clumsiest.

BRADLEY. Maybe that's my charm.

BRENDA. We haven't established that you have any charm. You're gonna make me a star.

BRADLEY. I could.

BRENDA. Fuck you.

BRADLEY. Fuck you.

BRENDA. Fuck you.

BRADLEY. Fuck you. Good. Now that we've established a common language, what do you think?

BRENDA. I've got Victor.

BRADLEY. And I've got the movie.

BRENDA. It's the director's movie.

BRADLEY. But the director is weak.

BRENDA. You say.

BRADLEY. You know I'm right.

BRENDA. And Collette?

BRADLEY. Is a dead, plastic mistake.

BRENDA. Dustin isn't going to give you any money.

BRADLEY. No harm in asking.

BRENDA. That's not so.

BRADLEY. All right, that's true. You ask Dustin, he says yes, you've used up your one big chit. You ask him, he says no, you find out you never had a chit. But lemme ask you this. Do you think you're a good actress?

BRENDA. Yes.

BRADLEY. If you got the shot, do you think you could make

America love you?

BRENDA. What's a Completion Bond Company?

BRADLEY. Who the fuck have you been talking to?!

BRENDA. Some Teamsters.

BRADLEY. That's a company seizes control of a picture if it goes too far over budget.

BRENDA. Is that what's going to happen to this picture?

BRADLEY. Not while I'm alive.

BRENDA. How's your health? How would Victor change the script to make it for me?

BRADLEY. We'd focus more on your feelings. Maybe some voice-overs over your face, your thoughts.

BRENDA. I have a better idea.

BRADLEY. You do?

BRENDA. Let me save Johnny.

BRADLEY. But Johnny dies!

BRENDA. Why?

BRADLEY. It's the big scene!

BRENDA. It'd be a bigger scene if he lived. And I saved him. And you cut Collette down but not out, and she was the one who set him up.

BRADLEY. So you get the guy.

BRENDA. I get the guy.

BRADLEY. How romantic. I don't know if it's a better ending, but it's better for you.

BRENDA. It's better.

BRADLEY. You talked to Victor about this?

BRENDA. A little bit.

BRADLEY. You chant for it?

BRENDA. Constantly.

BRADLEY. Should we have a drink? *(He is already pouring a glass for himself.)*

BRENDA. You go ahead.

BRADLEY. Doesn't jibe with your beliefs?

BRENDA. When I'm near the thing I want, I shouldn't blow it over a margarita.

BRADLEY. What do you want?

BRENDA. I want to be famous.

BRADLEY. Why?

BRENDA. I don't know. Is Collette really bad in the part?

BRADLEY. I don't know. I don't know anything about acting.

BRENDA. Neither do I. But I'm good.

BRADLEY. Can I ask you something?

BRENDA. You're the producer.

BRADLEY. What does that mean? You're good?

BRENDA. It's the bottom quality. I can't explain it.

BRADLEY. You really do come across on film. Vivid.

BRENDA. That's all I care about.

BRADLEY. I guess that's why the camera likes you. You're faithful.

BRENDA. Are you going to get George fired?

BRADLEY. I would lay down my life for George Lee Beech.

BRENDA. You just finished saying he was a weak director.

BRADLEY. That's right, he is. He's also the guy who gave me this shot when nobody else would. He made it possible for me to come back as a film producer, producing a Go Picture, on the streets of New York. I think he saved my marriage. My wife hates L.A. She says the water's hard. I know he saved my career after the indictment. I kind of think he saved my life. I don't give a fuck about this movie except as it detracts from or enhances the career of George Lee Beech. He's been the best to me that any man has ever been. What do I care if he's weak? That he drinks too much? That he's deeply influenced by whoever he spoke to last? Every picture has its reality. The reality of this picture is the director is weak and there's like five people fighting for control.

BRENDA. I count four.

BRADLEY. Everybody wants to be an artist. If there's a chance to stamp, everybody wants to jump in and make it *their* fuckin' stamp. But this project is going to fly to pieces unless some kind of coalition of principals, or demi-principals, agrees to some kind of direction.

BRENDA. What you're talking about is cutting off George's balls.

BRADLEY. That was taken care of long ago, honey. What

16

I'm trying to do is save what's left of George. Out of gratitude. And save what's left of this picture so we all look good.

BRENDA.   I'm not gonna ask Dustin for money.

BRADLEY.   Why not?

BRENDA.   Because you don't need it. You just think you need it. Producers always think the answer's money 'cause money's all they know.

BRADLEY.   We need money.

BRENDA.   We need Victor to cut thirteen scenes, rewrite two, and write two new ones.

BRADLEY.   Two new ones for you.

BRENDA.   For me.

BRADLEY.   How nice. Now rewind. Cut what thirteen scenes.

BRENDA.   We don't need the car crash.

BRADLEY.   You're sure?

BRENDA.   Yeah. We don't need the helicopter shot, therefore we don't need the gyrosphere or that gyrosphere operator. We don't need the character of Helen. And we don't need the effects at all.

BRADLEY.   My niece is playing Helen.

BRENDA.   I know. I didn't say there wasn't going to be blood on the floor.

BRADLEY.   When did you figure all this out?

BRENDA.   I chanted about it.

BRADLEY.   If we don't need the effects, we don't need the helicopter and we don't need Helen, then you're about right. We don't need money. But does George have a movie?

BRENDA.   He has a better movie. And you know that union guy who comes in at the end and makes the big speech? I think my step-brother should play that part. And if I ask him, I think he would.

BRADLEY.   That would be incredible. His face in the trailer would be worth at least one million ...

BRENDA.   *(Stepping on his line.)* So, are we like, in league?

BRADLEY.   What about Victor?

BRENDA.   I don't know yet. I mean, what the best way is to get him to do what needs to be done. I'll have to chant about it.

BRADLEY. All right. I'm in. Lemme ask you something. This is your first movie.

BRENDA. Right.

BRADLEY. How do you have like this ferocious bite on the script where you know, or you think you know, exactly what needs to be done to it?

BRENDA. I had William Goldman read it and analyze it for me.

BRADLEY. WILLIAM GOLDMAN! How did you get William Goldman?!

BRENDA. He wrote my brother's first movie. I've known him since I was a kid.

BRADLEY. William Goldman! Jesus!

BRENDA. Well, you're impressed.

BRADLEY. William Goldman! He's a Cannes judge. He's a Miss America judge for Chrissake. He's a giant. You've got his notes on our script?

BRENDA. Ten pages single space.

BRADLEY. Can I see them?

BRENDA. No.

BRADLEY. Why not?

BRENDA. I don't agree with all of them.

BRADLEY. You don't.... This is the guy who wrote *Butch Cassidy*. This is the guy who wrote *All the President's Men*. This is the guy who wrote *Tootsie*, for Chrissake.

BRENDA. He didn't write *Tootsie*.

BRADLEY. So what! I bet they offered it to him. You know what I mean my point. Who are you to even *read* this man's notes?

BRENDA. You know what your problem is?

BRADLEY. What?

BRENDA. Low self-esteem.

BRADLEY. That's true. How did you know that?

BRENDA. Just do yourself a favor and follow my lead.

BRADLEY. God, I'm so physically uncomfortable! I'm sorry!

BRENDA. What's the matter?

BRADLEY. Well, this is kind of disgusting.

BRENDA. What are you talking about?

BRADLEY. I've got a strange problem.

BRENDA. What?

BRADLEY. I've got a ... on my rectum ... I've got a surface ulcer, a canker, the size of a jumbo shrimp.

BRENDA. Really?

BRADLEY. It just keeps getting bigger.

BRENDA. What causes a thing like that?

BRADLEY. I don't know.

BRENDA. Been to the doctor?

BRADLEY. Not till this film's in the can.

BRENDA. I admire your commitment.

BRADLEY. I keep changing the dressing, but I just can't seem to keep it dry.

BRENDA. You mean sweat?

BRADLEY. No. It's runny. It runs.

BRENDA. Oh.

BRADLEY. And it has a smell, a fetid odor.

BRENDA. Really.

BRADLEY. Needless to say it hasn't been too romantic for my marriage. I know it's an actualization of my fear.

BRENDA. What are you afraid of?

BRADLEY. Everything's interrelated. My marriage and George and this movie.

BRENDA. You should get clear then, because those are all different things.

BRADLEY. How do you know? (*She writes something down and pushes it across to him.*)

BRENDA. Here.

BRADLEY. What's this?

BRENDA. You should call that number.

BRADLEY. What is it?

BRENDA. A holy man.

BRADLEY. Is this the chap that got you chanting?

BRENDA. That's right.

BRADLEY. No thanks.

BRENDA. You'll call that number if you wanna get rid of that physical problem, Bradley. This guy can dry up your sore.

BRADLEY. Do you find me repulsive?

19

BRENDA. Are you coming on to me?

BRADLEY. No.

BRENDA. I didn't think so.

BRADLEY. I would never do anything to jeopardize my third marriage. Do you think I could go out and get a FOURTH nice young woman to marry me? The world is not that big. No. I've got to keep my record to where it is: Two divorces, but the third marriage is a Go. It works. Have you ever been married?

BRENDA. Not really. Briefly. Twice.

BRADLEY. Then you know what I'm talking about. Maybe I will call him.

BRENDA. Do it.

BRADLEY. What's the time frame on Victor?

BRENDA. You tell me.

BRADLEY. If he makes the changes, and the changes are right, and the changes are as extensive as you describe, then George has got to read it Thursday, approve, so that I can do a major production meeting Friday, make projections, talk to the money people over the weekend, and jump into a new schedule on Monday morning.

BRENDA. So we have four days.

BRADLEY. You have four days. I'm going to get those scenes cut with you or without you. But if I have to do it without you, I'm not protecting your part.

BRENDA. But you said I'm better than Collette!

BRADLEY. I don't know anything about acting! I don't care anything about acting! I know that this movie is too long and too expensive and I'll be god damned if I'm going to let the Completion Bond Company come in and savage what's left of George Lee Beech's career! Do you understand me?

BRENDA. Yes.

BRADLEY. I don't give a fuck about you except insofar as you aid and abet me in my goals! If you can powder your own ass at the same time, good for you! I won't stand in your way. But don't kid yourself, Brenda! You can drop names and seem certain and pitch a plan of attack better than Julius Caesar, but if Victor doesn't come through on your notes, then you're just another piece of meat to me, right?

BRENDA.   Right.

BRADLEY.   I've seen it all before. I've been impressed before. It don't mean nothing. I'm free inside. GOD DAMMIT MY ASS IS KILLING ME! IT'S DRIVING ME NUTS! What is this fucking curse! JESUS!

BRENDA.   Call that number.

BRADLEY.   FUCK YOU! GET OUTTA HERE! I've got work to do. *(She gets up and goes.)* What a case. *(He looks at the number she gave him, crushes it, and tosses it. He hits the intercom.)* Get me Bill Goldman. *(Blackout.)*

Scene 2

A smoky bar. Collette drinks. Victor enters from the gloom with a drink.

VICTOR.   Collette, Collette.

COLLETTE.   Victor, hi. How you doin'?

VICTOR.   You're alone?

COLLETTE.   Can you believe they sat me at a table for six?

VICTOR.   In this dump you deserve a table for ten. I thought Brenda might be here.

COLLETTE.   She left.

VICTOR.   So I missed her.

COLLETTE.   She had to go. She has a call tomorrow.

VICTOR.   I know. I've been writing scenes on the back of the call sheet.

COLLETTE.   You're writing new scenes?

VICTOR.   I'm tinkerin', toyin'. Who knows what'll come of it.

COLLETTE.   It's a great script. It's so chunky.

VICTOR.   Tell that to the producers. Bradley is on my back.

COLLETTE.   What about?

VICTOR.   Length.

COLLETTE.   You have beautiful hair.

VICTOR. I do?

COLLETTE. Brenda's in love with you, you know.

VICTOR. Get outta here! Brenda's not in love with me!

COLLETTE. You should hear her in the trailer. Victor, Victor, Victor.

VICTOR. I don't have to hear her. I know she's not in love with me.

COLLETTE. How?

VICTOR. She doesn't even know me.

COLLETTE. Who does know you?

VICTOR. My agent.

COLLETTE. Ooo you're tough. So what scenes are you foolin' around with?

VICTOR. I had to fill out this form today. And I hadda name a beneficiary. I put down my agent.

COLLETTE. I hadda fill out that form. I put my mother.

VICTOR. I wouldn't put my mother! *(A pause.)*

COLLETTE. You know I've really come to love Brenda. She's so sweet.

VICTOR. She chants all the time.

COLLETTE. She says it saved her life. And you know I believe her. She comes from a very screwy background.

VICTOR. I know.

COLLETTE. I mean her brother lives in a car.

VICTOR. I know, I know, and her mother lived in a box. *(A pause.)*

COLLETTE. I'm attracted to you.

VICTOR. Oh. I'm flattered. You're an attractive woman.

COLLETTE. Thank you. *(A pause.)*

VICTOR. It's getting late.

COLLETTE. I can sleep in tomorrow.

VICTOR. I know you live with Mark so I guess you …

COLLETTE. *(Cutting him off.)* Yeah. Do you believe I'm attracted to you?

VICTOR. I'd better go.

COLLETTE. Don't go. Do you believe I'm attracted to you?

VICTOR. You don't pick up on signals, do you?

COLLETTE. I've always preferred English. Do you believe

I'm attracted to you?

VICTOR.   OKAY, COLLETTE, FORGIVE ME, I BELIEVE YOU WANT TO SUCK MY DICK!

COLLETTE.   Huh? What? What did you say to me?!

VICTOR.   Well, that's what you're talking about, right?

COLLETTE.   No, that's not what I was talking about!

VICTOR.   Come on, Collette! You're not talking about reading poetry. I'm seeing Brenda, who you think is so wonderful and amusing! You're living with Mark, Mister Jealous, I can't blame him, it's two o'clock in the morning and Donde esta Usted?! I've hadda enough to drink where if you ripped out my gall bladder I might not miss it! We're in some ragass scuzbucket theatre bar where I can smell the disinfectant in the bathroom OUT HERE! You're looking into my eyes. Under these conditions, forgive me, I figure you wanna suck my dick. Am I wrong?

COLLETTE.   Yes you are wrong!

VICTOR.   I don't think so.

COLLETTE.   What's happening to you, Victor?

VICTOR.   Fair question, tough question, I don't know. Now, don't get me wrong, Collette. I don't think you wanna suck my dick because you *actually* want to suck my dick! I think you wanna suck my dick to fuck over your friend colleague compadre BRENDA, who you love so much, or you wanna suck my dick to undermine the manhood of your live-in, MARK, the well-named. Some motive in that arena. I hope you believe me when I tell you it never occurred to me that you actually wanted to suck my dick for the JOY of sucking my dick. I guess I'm not a romantic. I used to be. Prior to joining the Writer's Guild. JESUS FUCKING CHRIST I WISH THIS DRINK TASTED BETTER!

COLLETTE.   Who do you think you are?

VICTOR.   Me? I'm nobody! That much is clear. I feel that keenly and acutely. I'm nobody nothin', my faith in life is sapped.

COLLETTE.   Had a bad day?

VICTOR.   Words cannot describe. I had a very bad day.

COLLETTE.   How much did you drink?

VICTOR. Tonight?

COLLETTE. Tonight.

VICTOR. Including breakfast?

COLLETTE. Leave out the eggs.

VICTOR. Thanks for reminding me. *(Produces an egg.)* Hard boiled, like me. Counting everything I drank a great deal. A GREAT deal. I was hoping to see Brenda. And as it happens, I like to tighten my rivets before I fly that patch of sky.

COLLETTE. You hide your liquor pretty good. I can't even tell you're drunk. Except by what you say.

VICTOR. You shall know me by what I say. Writers drink.

COLLETTE. Not all writers drink.

VICTOR. True. Hacks go into rehab. Good writers drink.

COLLETTE. So if Brenda doesn't love you because Brenda doesn't even know you, what are you doing coming around looking for Brenda?

VICTOR. I like the way she looks.

COLLETTE. And why you so hostile to me?

VICTOR. 'Cause you're dangling bait and if I rose to the bait you'd play out this fucking tragedy on my time bout your life. In short, you're an actress.

COLLETTE. Brenda's an actress.

VICTOR. Brenda is not an actress. She's a personality.

COLLETTE. You must like me.

VICTOR. Why?

COLLETTE. To talk to me this way.

VICTOR. I trust you in the sense I feel I know who I'm talking to.

COLLETTE. You talk this way to Brenda?

VICTOR. No. With her it's lofty. It's a loftier deal. *(Collette leans back, pleased.)*

COLLETTE. So let me get this straight. Do you think ... that there's no woman who wants to suck your dick with no motive but to suck your dick?

VICTOR. None.

COLLETTE. Well, you're probably right.

VICTOR. Thanks.

COLLETTE. And does this make you gloomy?

VICTOR.   If you're asking me how I feel, I don't know how I feel about anything.

COLLETTE.   I know that's not true.

VICTOR.   Anything to do with sex.

COLLETTE.   That I believe.

VICTOR.   I hope I remember this conversation tomorrow. Not the gist. The details. They say God is in the details.

COLLETTE.   I wish He'd show up in some of the broader strokes. Nobody wants to suck anybody's dick just to suck their dick.

VICTOR.   No?

COLLETTE.   It's not just you. Everything's about something else.

VICTOR.   What's this conversation about? *(Sees somebody real or imagined.)* AND WHO THE FUCK ARE YOU LOOKING AT?!

COLLETTE.   Be cool. This is the last place I can get this chicken. This exchange is about show business.

VICTOR.   Oh, go home!

COLLETTE.   You're drifting outta the circle, Shakespeare. You'd better be careful.

VICTOR.   What circle?

COLLETTE.   The circle of acquaintance. The society circle. You could find yourself more alone than you already are.

VICTOR.   Who asked you?

COLLETTE.   You could find yourself gettin' a dog and givin' up on people and then fallin' out with your dog.

VICTOR.   Are you tryin' to scare me?

COLLETTE.   I don't have to scare you, you're spooked.

VICTOR.   That's what you're doing. You're trying to scare me into fucking you!

COLLETTE.   Scared straight, huh?

VICTOR.   That's right. That's good. Well, it's all right.

COLLETTE.   If I just wanted to fuck you, I could just fuck you. Men are easy.

VICTOR.   How do you do it?

COLLETTE.   You just keep trying. Sooner or later, they have a bad day.

VICTOR. Well, if you don't wanna fuck me ...

COLLETTE. JUST fuck you.

VICTOR. If you don't wanna *just* fuck me, what do you want?

COLLETTE. You promise never to tell anybody about what I'm saying?

VICTOR. Promise.

COLLETTE. Because I want to be unrestrained.

VICTOR. Me too! That's all I want!

COLLETTE. I can talk to you in an open agendaless way if you're agendaless.

VICTOR. But you have an agenda!

COLLETTE. I have stated agendas and I'm hinting at an unstated agenda, but I ain't saying another fucking thing unless you promise ...

VICTOR. I did promise!

COLLETTE. All right then. What if Johnny lives?

VICTOR. What?

COLLETTE. At the end of the movie now, Johnny dies. But what if Johnny lives?

VICTOR. Johnny can't live!

COLLETTE. Why not?

VICTOR. How could he live?

COLLETTE. I could save him.

VICTOR. But you'd have to think about what that would mean.

COLLETTE. I have thought about it.

VICTOR. It's not that kind of picture.

COLLETTE. You're right. Right now it's an Art House Picture.

VICTOR. It is not an Art House Picture!

COLLETTE. The guy dies, everything falls apart, life stinks. It's an Art House Picture.

VICTOR. This is going to open in at least six hundred theatres.

COLLETTE. For a week.

VICTOR. What do you mean, for a week?!

COLLETTE. It'll last a week. Unless Johnny lives. You're a

terrific writer, Victor, but you're not Aeschylus. When Johnny dies, it's not a tragedy. It's just a fuckin' bummer.

VICTOR.   Nobody agrees with you.

COLLETTE.   Don't be so sure about that.

VICTOR.   They're talking about cuts, but nobody's talking about the ending.

COLLETTE.   That's 'cause it's later in the shoot. Now they'll be after you for cuts. Later they'll be after you for this focockda ending.

VICTOR.   You can't talk to me like this.

COLLETTE.   It's amazing what offends some people.

VICTOR.   George likes the end.

COLLETTE.   George? Hey, they roll George around on wheels I think.

VICTOR.   He's very smart.

COLLETTE.   So was Hamlet, but I don't think he woulda made a good movie director. You know what you don't seem to understand, Victor? This is your ass.

VICTOR.   I know that.

COLLETTE.   You know that. Right. So I take it back. It's not your ass. It's my ass. Think of my ass.

VICTOR.   I'd rather not.

COLLETTE.   I'll get you for that.

VICTOR.   Look, this is more important to me than anybody. This is my first movie.

COLLETTE.   That's right! It's your first movie, and they'll take that into account if it turns out to be a fuckin' mess that goes straight to video!

VICTOR.   No way is this film going straight to video! It's opening in minimum six hundred screens! It's a major picture, for Chrissake! It's a Disney Picture!

COLLETTE.   It's not a Disney picture.

VICTOR.   Disney's distributing this picture.

COLLETTE.   You've got a distribution deal?

VICTOR.   It's a negative pick-up.

COLLETTE.   IF they like it.

VICTOR.   They'll like it.

COLLETTE.   If Johnny lives they'll like it.

VICTOR.   JOHNNY CAN'T LIVE!

COLLETTE.   This is your first picture, Victor. It's unfair of me to expect that you'd understand how things are very clear to me. I've done six pictures. Where the parts mattered. This is my last ingenue.

VICTOR.   Ingenue? I wouldn't call that part an ingenue.

COLLETTE.   What would you call it?

VICTOR.   I don't know ... in terms of the plot, it's ...

COLLETTE.   I wouldn't have taken this part if it wasn't an ingenue. It's an ingenue. That was a contract point.

VICTOR.   It's in your contract that you're an ingenue?

COLLETTE.   When they made me the offer, they offered me the ingenue.

VICTOR.   They didn't use the character name?

COLLETTE.   No, they used the character name, but they used the character name of the ingenue, because it's the ingenue role!

VICTOR.   What does it matter anyway?

COLLETTE.   It matters to me! I'm the ingenue!

VICTOR.   All right. You're the ingenue.

COLLETTE.   Thank you. Anyway, my next trip out, I'm the lead or I'm a character actress. This is the fork in the road for me.

VICTOR.   They screwed me out of twenty-five thousand dollars today. I was supposed to get this fee for associate producing and they held me up for it. Said I wouldn't be welcome on the set if I demanded my contract.

COLLETTE.   If this movie plays a week and goes to video, I'm a character actress from here on. Somebody's aunt, somebody's crying sister. If this movie gets major distribution ...

VICTOR.   I told you! Disney's distributing this picture!

COLLETTE.   Victor, you don't know anything. You're whistling in the dark. Would you listen to me?

VICTOR.   Johnny can't live!

COLLETTE.   There are forces at work here. Many forces. DARK forces. Certain things are going to happen. You can make them happen, or they can happen to you. Do you want this picture to get picked up by Disney?

VICTOR. Yes.

COLLETTE. If this picture gets major distribution, I'm not a character actress, I'm a lead. What do you think I want to be in my next picture, somebody's aunt with cancer, or the lead?

VICTOR. The lead.

COLLETTE. That's right. So you and I want the same thing. We want people to like this picture.

VICTOR. I don't want everybody to like this picture.

COLLETTE. Don't worry, you're covered. All right. So. I come in. He's on the point of death ...

VICTOR. JOHNNY CAN'T LIVE!

COLLETTE. All right, what are you trying to say with Johnny's death?

VICTOR. Do you think that Brenda really likes me?

COLLETTE. God! You're asking me? Didn't you sleep with her?

VICTOR. Yeah, but ...

COLLETTE. Couldn't you tell anything from that?

VICTOR. Sort've.

COLLETTE. So she likes you, right?

VICTOR. Well, no, that's not exactly what I got.

COLLETTE. No?

VICTOR. I didn't feel she was really there.

COLLETTE. Well, you ask a lot.

VICTOR. I felt, in a way, like a Polynesian god receiving a human sacrifice.

COLLETTE. Shine a light, Victor. How do you mean?

VICTOR. She submitted to a grim fate for a higher purpose.

COLLETTE. Wow. Well. Let's talk about the movie.

VICTOR. I don't want to.

COLLETTE. Why not?

VICTOR. I'm bored with talking about the movie.

COLLETTE. So what?

VICTOR. I'm just really bored with it.

COLLETTE. So what? That goes without saying. I'm so bored I wish someone would come in here and take a gun my fuckin' brains on the floor. I'm so bored I might e in jail, in solitary with a leaky tin cup and a book an't read. I'm so schizoid bored, bug-eyed, stultified past hope that I'm sitting here talking to you, Victor, ou've gotta be the zonker fuckin' ennui king of walking deaᴜdom!

VICTOR. Who?!

COLLETTE. You. You are the Chief! You are the floor model! A fit subject for Mister Sammy Beckett on a bad, bad day!

VICTOR. Who's drifting outta the circle now?

COLLETTE. It's not such a great circle anyway.

VICTOR. Maybe I'm going home.

COLLETTE. Don't go home! What's home like?

VICTOR. Well, everything's filthy. Maybe I won't go home.

COLLETTE. Why would you? I shudder when I think of going home. I got this guy in my apartment. Mark. I'm supposed to marry him. Some days. He hates me. He waits up for me no matter how late it gets so he can scream at me and accuse me of horrendous shit that I have in fact done. We fuck, it's great, and then I tell him I didn't feel anything. Nobody cooks. Food rots. Fruit flies abound. You see what I'm drivin' at, Victor?!

VICTOR. I don't know what the fuck you're talking about.

COLLETTE. Yes, you do! OH YES YOU DO! I'm talking about the LIFE! This is the LIFE! You're not gonna break through in your apartment! You're gonna break through in your career, in a BIG way, or sink into the muck of your rotting, neglected, private existence!

VICTOR. Why do you hate Mark so much?

COLLETTE. Because he gave me pleasure when I wanted to be badly disappointed. You've got to focus, Victor! Everybody else is totally focused and you're wandering around wondering if the girls really like you! Don't you get it? Nobody cares about you! Nobody can even see you! We're scratchin' for our lives down here! Who are you to toy with my career? I hate it that I can't just take out a shotgun and blow your brains out! Why is that wrong? And George! That puppet!

And that airhead Brenda! And that creepy Bradley! Oh, that I should be in the hands of such people! What do you want, Victor? What will it take for you to do the decent thing? Help me save this picture! Help me, or take this knife and stop the fuckin' pain! I can't believe I started off as a little girl! At this point, I feel like I hatched out of a leathery egg in some stinking bog in the Congo!

VICTOR. Maybe you should have some coffee.

COLLETTE. What happened to me? What happened to my innocence? Look at me! I used to be pretty!

VICTOR. You are pretty.

COLLETTE. Thank you.

VICTOR. It's true.

COLLETTE. Johnny lives. Let Johnny live. Let me save Johnny. I'm begging you. Of course you can sleep with me. Only too glad.

VICTOR. I'm sorry. It goes against my instincts.

COLLETTE. What, saving Johnny or sleeping with me?

VICTOR. Both.

COLLETTE. Your instincts? Don't you have the instinct of self-preservation? Don't you understand that they're going to crush you on this shoot if you get in their way? Today they got you for twenty-five grand. You didn't think they could do that, did you? You hadda contract. But they got you anyway. And they'll get you again! And again! Till there's nothing left. Some buzzards. Some bones. The picture'll be done. Johnny will live. Somebody will save him. Probably not me. Have you been going to dailies?

VICTOR. Yeah.

COLLETTE. How am I?

VICTOR. You're great.

COLLETTE. Do I look fat?

VICTOR. No.

COLLETTE. Is my accent good?

VICTOR. Pretty good. It could be a little less ...

COLLETTE. *(Stepping on the line.)* Oh, what the fuck do you know!

VICTOR. Sorry. I guess I don't know anything. You're right.

Everybody else is focused, and I'm ... I close my eyes, and I see how I feel, and I try to do that. That's what's always worked for me. What else do I have? I could listen to you or Brenda or Bradley or George, but then I'd just be lost. I mean, aren't you lost, Collette?

COLLETTE.   Yes.

VICTOR.   Don't you know that you're lost?

COLLETTE.   I do know that.

VICTOR.   You may be focused, but on what?

COLLETTE.   Stayin' out of the rain.

VICTOR.   There's more to life than that.

COLLETTE.   Not when you're wet.

VICTOR.   There's always more to life than that.

COLLETTE.   How would you know? You're drunk.

VICTOR.   Writers drink.

COLLETTE.   Yes, they do.

VICTOR.   I can see what you must've been like when you were a little girl.

COLLETTE.   Still tryin' to be liked.

VICTOR.   What's the matter with you?

COLLETTE.   I know too much, and you're too big a fool. You overwhelm me. I can't talk to you. You're like a toddler. Thinkin' you're standin' on your own, people all around you holdin' you up. Victor, I'm sorry. I'm desperate. I'm going to have to come against you obliquely. Through the system. Like septic shock.

VICTOR.   What are you talking about?

COLLETTE.   You leave me no choice. I tried to do the honorable course, but you are a dry riverbed.

VICTOR.   You know, you're drunk.

COLLETTE.   Yeah, but the difference is tomorrow.... Oh, never mind. Sentimental writer.

VICTOR.   My writing is not sentimental.

COLLETTE.   Not your writing. You.

VICTOR.   You know this whole way of working, this system. It doesn't have to be this way.

COLLETTE.   Oh yes it does. It has its own peculiar genius.

VICTOR.   My mother died today.

COLLETTE.   What?

VICTOR.   My mother died today. That's why I put my agent as beneficiary.

COLLETTE.   My God, I'm sorry.

VICTOR.   I wasn't going to tell anyone. Maybe I would've told Brenda, but I couldn't find her. I didn't want to tell anyone. Get it mixed up with all this lousy other stuff!

COLLETTE.   I can't believe it.

VICTOR.   There's nothing you can do. There's nothing I can do. I wish could feel her arms around me one more time.

COLLETTE.   Yes.

VICTOR.   I can feel where her hands would be. Everyone I'm dealing with now is so cold!

COLLETTE.   I know. It's ...

VICTOR.   This business is so hard! Heartless. I was going to call her just to unburden myself. I put off the call. And today, they told me she was dead.

COLLETTE.   Was she sick?

VICTOR.   No. She just.... It was just sudden. So when you say, like in the movie, that this guy should be saved at the last minute ... I mean the heartbreak of life is real! I feel it! I feel it right now. My mother is dead. More than ever I've got to express that. For my salvation as a man. There's grief in the world. I feel it. This has just been the most awful experience, Collette. The one person in the world I knew loved me is dead.

COLLETTE.   I feel for you, Victor. But I still think Johnny should live. *(Blackout.)*

ACT TWO

Scene 1

A small makeup trailer on a location film set. A window with drawn blinds. Brenda is rocking and chanting. Collette enters, hungover.

COLLETTE. Brenda. Brenda. Brenda. Brenda!
BRENDA. Did you say something?
COLLETTE. No.
BRENDA. How's my wig?
COLLETTE. What wig?
BRENDA. This wig on my head.
COLLETTE. It's you.
BRENDA. I look like Daisy Duck.
COLLETTE. No.
BRENDA. Tell me the truth. I look like Samantha on *Bewitched.*
COLLETTE. You look fine.
BRENDA. I look innocent?
COLLETTE. You look innocent.
BRENDA. I'm so nervous.
COLLETTE. Why?
BRENDA. You know, today's my first real scene. Dialogue scene.
COLLETTE. Piece a cake.
BRENDA. You don't have to worry because you're so good. If I had the kind of skills and talent you do, I'd be cool, too.
COLLETTE. Can I ask you something?
BRENDA. What?
COLLETTE. What is it you chant?
BRENDA. Oh, you know, I can't tell you that.
COLLETTE. Oh.
BRENDA. That was part of my orientation. That I couldn't say.

COLLETTE. That's all right. I think I kinda know anyway.

BRENDA. You do?

COLLETTE. I think so.

BRENDA. How could you know?

COLLETTE. Well, I listen to you do it, you know.

BRENDA. Oh, I'm sorry! I'm driving you crazy.

COLLETTE. No. I can get used to anything. That's my strength.

BRENDA. That's funny.

COLLETTE. Why?

BRENDA. That's my strength, too. I never found Victor last night.

COLLETTE. No?

BRENDA. I went to Orso's. He never showed up.

COLLETTE. Really?

BRENDA. You're sure he said Orso's?

COLLETTE. Pretty sure. So. I could make out your chant, but I can't for the life a me figure why you'd chant something like that.

BRENDA. Couldn't you?

COLLETTE. Uncle Remus. What good could it do to say Uncle Remus over and over again?

BRENDA. Well, you know it doesn't matter what you say.

COLLETTE. But Uncle Remus over and over again? At first I thought it was funny, but Jesus Christ I mean ...

BRENDA. I don't say Uncle Remus!

COLLETTE. You don't?

BRENDA. I say, I am famous. (Pause.) I really needed to talk to Victor last night. I was desperate to talk to him. That's one of the reasons I'm nervous now. I had like a problem with my character — and it's in this scene, too. I felt like if I could talk it out with him, maybe he could help me or fix it or something. But now, you know, we're gonna shoot it, and it's so irrevocable. Where is he?

COLLETTE. Victor is a very difficult writer.

BRENDA. I don't think so.

COLLETTE. He is.

BRENDA. Why do you say that?

COLLETTE. I saw him last night.

BRENDA. What?

COLLETTE. I sent you off on a wild goose to Orso's so I could have Victor alone and have a talk with him.

BRENDA. I'm stunned.

COLLETTE. He's not here today probably because he was very drunk and he's probably home sleeping it off.

BRENDA. This is the kind of thing.... This kind of thing is the reason I left L.A.

COLLETTE. It is?

BRENDA. You deceived me.

COLLETTE. Yes.

BRENDA. You bitch.

COLLETTE. You wanna talk to me that way I can talk to you that way. You fucking cow.

BRENDA. Why did you lie to me?

COLLETTE. You're lucky I didn't just get you fired.

BRENDA. You don't have that power.

COLLETTE. Maybe not.

BRENDA. What did you say to Victor?

COLLETTE. A lot of things. A few of which I remember.

BRENDA. Did you sleep with him?

COLLETTE. I offered, but the logistics were bad. No, you had knowledge of him first, Brenda, but it's like some people say about you. You're not an actress, you're a personality. He didn't buy it.

BRENDA. What do you mean?

COLLETTE. Victor didn't believe that you were overcome with passion for him. You left him with a feeling of ashes. You know the feeling. I'm sure you have it every time you sleep with a man.

BRENDA. I don't have to listen to this.

COLLETTE. Absolutely not. Why don't you go back to Uncle Remus?

BRENDA. I don't say Uncle Remus!

COLLETTE. Oh, that's right. It's less nutty and more pathetic than that. I am famous.

BRENDA. I will be!

COLLETTE.   Maybe. With a lot of work. I mean facial sur-
gery. But it has a lot to do with luck you know. And your luck
isn't very good right now, Brenda.
BRENDA.   Why not?
COLLETTE.   Well. First of all, I see through you. Second of
all, Victor doesn't love you. And third of all, God is against
you.
BRENDA.   I'm a more spiritual person than you are, Collette.
I pray constantly.
COLLETTE.   You *chant* constantly. You say 'I am famous'
constantly. If God likes this in a person, that's His problem.
But you know I don't think he likes it. Because your first
scene is a walk-and-talk with Johnny, and it's really where your
whole character's established. It's a nice scene. It's an outdoor
scene. You're probably in the perfect emotional place to do
it. *(Pulls the blinds. Rain is thundering down.)* And it just started
pouring down fucking rain,
BRENDA.   RAIN! *(Collette laughs her dry, sardonic little laugh.)*
COLLETTE.   You know, I had a late call today. I coulda
slept in. But when I heard the weather report, I just hadda
be here.
BRENDA.   When's it gonna stop?
COLLETTE.   It's never gonna stop. Build a boat. Get a
hobby. It's never gonna stop.
BRENDA.   They'll just reschedule it.
COLLETTE.   Maybe they'll reschedule it. Maybe they'll de-
cide, in their money-grubbing, self-justifying little minds, that
they don't need that scene. That it's gratuitous.
BRENDA.   It is not gratuitous!
COLLETTE.   Maybe they'll decide you're gratuitous.
BRENDA.   What do you mean?
COLLETTE.   They do that, you know. They're superstitious.
They're fearful. They're ignorant as raw potato-sucking peas-
ants. I know these people. They're cattle. One loud noise and
they stampede.
BRENDA.   Why do you hate me?
COLLETTE.   I do hate you. Very well put.
BRENDA.   Why?

37

COLLETTE. Oh, I'm not as easy to understand as you, Brenda. Why strain your mind?

BRENDA. I want to know!

COLLETTE. I don't care to explain myself to you.

BRENDA. Bradley thinks you're lousy in the movie! He wants to cut you out!

COLLETTE. Really?

BRENDA. And I think he's right!

COLLETTE. Do you?

BRENDA. Bradley says you're a stage actress!

COLLETTE. Oh, I'm stung. So I'm too big, right?

BRENDA. Way too big! Grotesque! That's the word he used! They're laughing at you in dailies! He said, what you're doing, it's KABUKI!

COLLETTE. Well, that does hurt. Kabuki. When you put it that way. Do you have something, you know, when you're sick of all this, that you close your eyes and dream about?

BRENDA. What are you talking about?

COLLETTE. I don't know. I'm looking for something. A relaxing image to fall back on. A country cottage. A friendly manicurist. This could be a really good movie, you know?

BRENDA. What are these, just random thoughts?

COLLETTE. It won't be. I know that. Or if it is, it's just gonna be one of those strange monkey miracles that happen just often enough.... You know, if a monkey put it together and it turned out good. That's a monkey miracle. It happens sometimes. Just enough to give the monkeys hope.

BRENDA. What did you say to Victor last night?

COLLETTE. When did you talk to Bradley? *(No answer.)* That he was so forthcoming about my acting?

BRENDA. What did you say to Victor?

COLLETTE. That I thought Johnny should live.

BRENDA. What?

COLLETTE. I think Johnny should live.

BRENDA. You do?

COLLETTE. Yes.

BRENDA. But so do I.

COLLETTE. You do?

BRENDA. Yes.

COLLETTE. Why do you think Johnny should live?

BRENDA. Because it's too depressing if he dies. Because the whole movie's just a meaningless bummer if he's dead at the end.

COLLETTE. That's why I think Johnny should live. I don't like agreeing with you. It doesn't sit well. Who should save him? *(Brief pause.)*

BRENDA. You should.

COLLETTE. I should?

BRENDA. Yeah. *(Pause.)*

COLLETTE. Humm. Huh. Duh.

BRENDA. It doesn't matter that it's raining.

COLLETTE. Why not?

BRENDA. It's an insurance day. They have weather insurance against this kind of thing.

COLLETTE. How do you know that?

BRENDA. I know a lot about the movies.

COLLETTE. Oh, that's right. Your brother's in the business.

BRENDA. I don't like people to know that.

COLLETTE. Please. You trade on it.

BRENDA. He's my step-brother. *(Collette shrugs, then sings.)*

COLLETTE. It's raining, it's pouring,
The old man is snoring ...

BRENDA. It actually works in my favor that it's raining. Now Victor can fix the scene before we shoot it. So it tracks.

COLLETTE. So it tracks to what?

BRENDA. I'm just talking about character consistency.

COLLETTE. You wouldn't know character consistency if it bit you in the neck. Oh, duh, I get it. *You* want to save Johnny.

BRENDA. What?

COLLETTE. You save Johnny, you get the guy. It's your picture. So who am I? Oh, I'm the rat! I'm the rat who set him up! Then you can cut out half my scenes.

BRENDA. Three quarters.

COLLETTE. Victor would have to do a lot of work.

BRENDA. He'll do it.

COLLETTE.   Of course the movie would be a piece of shit then, but that's a side issue.

BRENDA.   Why's that?

COLLETTE.   'Cause then it's just a red herring movie. Oh, I thought it was her but it was HER. Pretty flat stuff. But in terms of career, very upper level. You get the guy, you trade up an agent, maybe you get one of those new faces articles. I had one of those.

BRENDA.   Six years ago.

COLLETTE.   You think you're a little brainy brain, don't you? I know you. I know the list you keep, I know your empty little heart. Every time I think I've fallen so low that I can't even lift my head and look at this face.... Every time I remember, WITH SHAME, that I was a child, and what I did with what I was given.... Every time I get afraid, and I really do get afraid, of what I've done with my life, and that there's no going back, there's no purgatory I can submit myself to to cauterize this ricotta cheese out of my soul ...

BRENDA.   You can't tell me ...

COLLETTE.   SHUT UP! I meet someone like you. And I stop worrying about myself. And I start worrying about the world. What's that smell?

BRENDA.   What?

COLLETTE.   There's some awful smell in here. *(She picks up a wastepaper basket.)* It's coming from here. What is that?

BRENDA.   Oh, I know what it is.

COLLETTE.   What?

BRENDA.   Bradley is always changing this dressing on this sore he's got. *(Collette drops the can.)*

COLLETTE.   Eww! What kind of sore?

BRENDA.   He's got this sore. It's on his BUTT!

COLLETTE.   Eww! Bradley was changing a dressing on his ass in our trailer?

BRENDA.   Yeah.

COLLETTE.   And you were here?

BRENDA.   Yeah.

COLLETTE.   And you let him?

BRENDA.   He was uncomfortable.

COLLETTE. Hey, you didn't …

BRENDA. What? No!

COLLETTE. I believe you.

BRENDA. Thank you.

COLLETTE. At least Victor is humanly presentable.

BRENDA. I think so.

COLLETTE. He just such a fuckin' puppy. I wanna kick him.

BRENDA. Oh, I wanna cuddle him! Something about him really touches me. And his work is so layered with levels …

COLLETTE. *(Stomps on her line.)* Comon, drop it, Brenda! It's lost on me!

BRENDA. Okay.

COLLETTE. We're getting along now. In a way. *(Brenda begins chanting.)* Don't chant.

BRENDA. Okay. What was the forecast?

COLLETTE. Perpetual rain. I can't believe they haven't shuttled us off to some cover set.

BRENDA. The A.D. said there was no cover today.

COLLETTE. You're kidding me! Geniuses. One of our parts is going to get cut to shit. If Johnny dies, both of our parts could get cut to shit.

BRENDA. Johnny can't die!

COLLETTE. All right. Johnny can't die. That's our platform.

BRENDA. And I want Victor.

COLLETTE. Victor is yours. After the shoot.

BRENDA. What am I going to do with him then? I want him now.

COLLETTE. You can't have him now. If you have Victor now, he'll tip the story to you and my stuff will end up on the floor. You get him after. If you want, you can have Bradley now.

BRENDA. I don't want Bradley!

COLLETTE. There might be some value in it for you.

BRENDA. I don't want him.

COLLETTE. Don't tell me you have a stomach that can be turned?

BRENDA. There's something about Bradley that makes me

feel really voodoo.

COLLETTE.   I know what you mean. He's one of those guys. He's got dead eyes.

BRENDA.   He said you have dead eyes. On film.

COLLETTE.   Why are you telling me these things that Bradley confided to you about me?

BRENDA.   If you offer me Bradley, then he mustn't be worth anything, so I guess I'm in league with you. Collette. We're friends.

COLLETTE.   Well, that's moving.

BRENDA.   My brother's baby-sitter used to have sex with him. I know that's like a guy's ultimate fantasy, a young guy anyway, but it really messed him up. I've been incested. By him. It's a chain. My father doesn't show his feelings. He's so like dead. I took care of him when he left my mother. We kept house. That was the happiest time in my life.

COLLETTE.   What happened? Did I accidentally hit a button?

BRENDA.   What do you mean?

COLLETTE.   You just said this whole thing out of nowhere.

BRENDA.   It came into my mind.

COLLETTE.   You said the exact same speech to me. In this trailer. Two weeks ago.

BRENDA.   Oh, I'm sorry.

COLLETTE.   So this is something you say.

BRENDA.   Yes, it is.

COLLETTE.   Why?

BRENDA.   It wins people over.

COLLETTE.   No it doesn't.

BRENDA.   Then I don't know why I do it.

COLLETTE.   You're like a beeping thing the space program sent out. Beep Beep Beep.

BRENDA.   I do not go Beep Beep Beep.

COLLETTE.   I've got a bulletin for you, Brenda. You're getting further and further from base.

BRENDA.   I do not go Beep Beep Beep.

COLLETTE.   No, you go I am famous, I am famous.

BRENDA.   I am going to be famous! I am going to chant

till I am famous or I am dead! I'm going to see this face in features! I'm going to hear this voice in Dolby! People are going to do slavish slave imitations of me!

COLLETTE.   Well, that's something to look forward to. You know what's really weird about this picture?

BRENDA.   What?

COLLETTE.   Nobody's even trying to sleep with the director.

BRENDA.   I did.

COLLETTE.   What happened?

BRENDA.   I did.

COLLETTE.   Oh. All right, let's talk script. And then we'll make our move. *(Collette picks up a blouse.)* Is this your blouse?

BRENDA.   Oh, yeah.

COLLETTE.   Good. *(Collette stuffs it in the garbage can.)* Really fine fabric is great for absorbing a smell.

BLACKOUT

Scene 2

The office. Rain falls steadily outside the one wide side window. Bradley, in a jacket, tie, and plastic white raincoat, looks moodily out the window. Someone knocks on the door. Bradley doesn't move. Again a knock and no response. Then Victor, in a dripping, shining black slicker, comes in.

VICTOR.   Well, what do you want?

BRADLEY.   *(Without moving.)* Rain.

VICTOR.   You had a production assistant come to my mother's wake, Bradley. This better be good. What do you want?

BRADLEY.   I fired the U.P.M.

VICTOR.   What's a U.P.M.?

BRADLEY.   The Unit Production Manager. It's an important job.

VICTOR.   Is it?

BRADLEY.   We don't have weather insurance.

VICTOR.   All right, what's weather insurance?

BRADLEY.   It means, if it rains, it's okay.

VICTOR.   So what did this guy do?   He didn't get the weather insurance?

BRADLEY.   No. I didn't get it. But. I can't fire myself. I can't do that to George. So I fired the U.P.M.

VICTOR.   OF WHAT, SIGNIFICANCE, IS THIS TO ME!
(Bradley seems to see Victor for the first time.)

BRADLEY.   Hi, Victor. How you doin'?

VICTOR.   NOT SO GOOD!   MY MOTHER'S DEAD!

BRADLEY.   We've got to cut ten scenes from this movie.

VICTOR.   I'm not cutting one fucking scene!

BRADLEY.   We're gonna lose this location after today. That's okay. It's just a walk-and-talk. But we're out seventy-five grand. The insurance glitch. That's a problem. Why don't you sit down. I can't.

VICTOR.   I don't want to sit down.

BRADLEY.   I know I screwed you out of twenty-five thousand dollars yesterday, Victor, but ...

VICTOR.   Yes, you did!

BRADLEY.   And I'll be honest with you. If I thought I could stick you for another twenty-five today, I would. I would take it from you. If I thought you had it on your person, I would knock you down and take it. I'm a desperate man. But remember this. I'm desperate for you.

VICTOR.   You misread the situation. I'm not desperate.

BRADLEY.   Oh yes you are! But you're not in touch with it. It's in you, but you're not feeling it. You're like George. George, at this point, is stupid with fear and weakness and exhaustion. But he doesn't know it. He thinks he feels fine. You know why?

VICTOR.   I'm not cutting one scene from this movie!

BRADLEY.   Because I'm protecting him and I'm protecting you by using my body as a host.

VICTOR.   Why don't you just rip the pages out of the script?! I don't have any contract protection! What do you need me for? Just let me go home and bury my mother. Call me for the wrap party.

BRADLEY. I can't let you go! I need you, Victor! Don't walk out that door! Listen. The director is weak! George is a great guy, but he's weak. He wants to be liked. He wants to be able to look in the mirror. He doesn't want to stomp on you like some others would do. If they were in charge. In a minute. He wants you to approve.

VICTOR. Approve what?

BRADLEY. Changes.

VICTOR. You mean you can't cut unless I say it's okay?

BRADLEY. That's right.

VICTOR. Well then, that's easy. I approve of no cuts, no changes, and I'm going home.

BRADLEY. Wait a minute, Victor! With power comes responsibility! There isn't enough money to shoot this whole script. There just isn't enough money.

VICTOR. For real?

BRADLEY. For real.

VICTOR. So what are you going to do? What's the scenario?

BRADLEY. Shoot till we go over budget. That triggers Completion Bond. Then they'll seize the picture. Slap what there is of it together. Voice-overs or something. It'll go straight to video. If it gets off the shelf.

VICTOR. Really?

BRADLEY. I've been alone with this. I could use a friend.

VICTOR. If you had a friend, you'd eat him.

BRADLEY. George Lee Beech is my friend.

VICTOR. And you're about halfway through him.

BRADLEY. I don't expect you to understand

VICTOR. Listen, I don't want to understand, but unfortunately I'm starting to.

BRADLEY. The one thing you don't see in this is yourself. That's understandable and dangerous. You're very inexperienced. You're from the theatre. That's like the Outback of entertainment. How'd you get to be in the movie business?

VICTOR. I'm a writer. I wrote a script.

BRADLEY. How come you didn't write another play? How

come you didn't write a novel?

VICTOR. I've been asking myself that.

BRADLEY. You know the answer. Money! Jing Jing. Money!

VICTOR. Yes.

BRADLEY. I work with money. Money is my life. Money's all I know, and there's only one thing I know about it. Money's just the smoke before you get to the bottom. Money's just confusion.

VICTOR. I don't think it's good to listen to you.

BRADLEY. Money's the place where morons stop and gape. Money isn't the root or flower of anything. You think you're in the movie business for the money, but nobody's in anything for the money. You were born to be in the business.

VICTOR. I was?

BRADLEY. Yes.

VICTOR. I don't think so.

BRADLEY. I know. It's my business to know. I would be useless to George Lee Beech unless I had this knowledge of people.

VICTOR. Where is George Lee Beech?

BRADLEY. Not far from here. In a hotel room. Resting till he's needed.

VICTOR. Why isn't he needed now? Why isn't he here telling me we're in big trouble and the script needs to be cut?

BRADLEY. Because it would endanger your and George's relationship.

VICTOR. What relationship? I never see George!

BRADLEY. Your future relationship.

VICTOR. You know, I'm just like amazed by something.

BRADLEY. What?

VICTOR. Why haven't I left this room?

BRADLEY. I'm gonna tell you a little story.

VICTOR. Oh, please don't.

BRADLEY. Once there was a great big pregnant bear.

VICTOR. Are you really doing this?

BRADLEY. And after a painful labor, she gave birth to seven baby bears.

VICTOR. Seven.

BRADLEY.   So she was very tired.

VICTOR.   Sure.

BRADLEY.   And she looked at her seven babies, and they were all gooey and slimy with afterbirth. And in that miraculous way that Nature has built the bear, she felt in her heart a tremendous welling up of material feeling.

VICTOR.   Maternal feeling.

BRADLEY.   Right. And this maternal feeling filled her with strength, so she licked and licked and licked her babies, one after the other, rendering them clean and fresh and beautiful. That is until she got to the seventh little bear. Right then, she ran out of gas, hadda seizure, and dropped dead. Muerto. And the six, well-tended little bears, with their beautiful brown coats, shed a tear, a tender tear, and bounded off into the woods. To have wonderful lives. And the seventh cub, the unlicked cub, went into show business.

VICTOR.   That's it?

BRADLEY.   That's it. Whenever I can't believe the behavior of somebody in the business, I think, this is an unlicked cub. Whenever I can't believe my behavior, I think, I am an unlicked cub. Being shocked, being taken aback, it's a waste of time. This is the way we are! This is the shithouse we're in! Let's get on with it!

VICTOR.   I'm not like you!

BRADLEY.   OH? HOW'S YOUR HOMELIFE?

VICTOR.   Fine!

BRADLEY.   Liar. But I expect you to lie. I don't mind. Relax. Lie. You can't help it. Just like a baboon can't help it that God painted his butt red. Now listen, Victor. If there's a power play now, you can take a stand and win. But what are you winning? A bad movie. With your name on it. *(Brenda throws open the door. She has no protection from the rain and she's drenched.)*

BRENDA.   Is it all right if I come in?

VICTOR.   Brenda, you're soaked.

BRENDA.   Oh, I'm fine.

BRADLEY.   An unlicked cub, Victor. Keep the image in your mind. It can be useful. *(To Brenda.)* I found out two things

47

about you, sweetie. You're not related to Dustin Murphy and you do not have notes from Bill Goldman. You don't even know Bill Goldman.

BRENDA.   I do know Bill Goldman!

BRADLEY.   How do you know Bill Goldman?

BRENDA.   I know his son!

BRADLEY.   Bill Goldman doesn't have a son.

BRENDA.   Yes, he does! He has a step-son!

BRADLEY.   Oh, we're back to the step-stuff! Lucky us! *(Hits the intercom.)* Get me Bill Goldman.

BRENDA.   All right!

BRADLEY.   *(To intercom.)* Forget it.

BRENDA.   My notes are still good!

VICTOR.   You have notes?

BRENDA.   Just some ideas.

BRADLEY.   Ten pages, single-spaced.

BRENDA.   I wanted to talk to you ...

BRADLEY.   You know, you're interrupting a meeting, Brenda ...

BRENDA.   But Collette told me you were going to be at Orso's.

BRADLEY.   I'll bet she did.

VICTOR.   Where'd she get that idea?

BRADLEY.   A matchbook. Listen, Victor, can I count on you not to be a big baby? Can I count on you to step forward like a man and cut this script down to something we can shoot?

VICTOR.   I know there's a problem with length, Bradley, and I wanna solve it, but I don't trust you!

BRENDA.   Why would you? He's a snake!

BRADLEY.   So I'm a snake! Don't trust me! Join the crowd! But notice the moment exclusive of me! Listen, Victor! Can you hear that whispering wind? It's a fateful breeze, Victor, very gentle and very rare. IT DOES NOT LAST. It brings words many long to hear and few do hear. It's the Picture talking. It's saying: Shoot me. Take me out and shoot me.

BRENDA.   I don't hear anything.

BRADLEY.   Don't ignore this breeze, Victor, and the words it brings. It blows for you today, but tomorrow, I promise you, it will muss somebody else's hair.

BRENDA. Is he talking in code?

BRADLEY. I'm talking to Victor. I'm talking about control. With cutting comes control.

VICTOR. Am I understanding you?

BRADLEY. You are understanding me.

VICTOR. I don't trust you.

BRADLEY. Don't trust me. Use me. Exploit me.

VICTOR. All right. I'll cut the script. All right.

BRADLEY. Now? Today?

VICTOR. Yeah.

BRENDA. What are you going to cut? You're not going to cut anything of mine, Victor, are you? *(She pulls out her notes.)* I have some ideas about one way you could condense ...

VICTOR. I think I know what to do.

BRADLEY. Good!

BRENDA. You do?

BRADLEY. Will you let the guy breathe!

BRENDA. Does Johnny live?

VICTOR. Yeah, Johnny lives.

BRENDA. He does?

VICTOR. Yeah. *(The door slams open again. A soaked Collette stands there.)*

COLLETTE. There you are!

BRADLEY. Here you go. Another unlicked cub.

BRENDA. Collette, Johnny lives!

COLLETTE. Did you think you were going to away with that?

BRENDA. Let me get you a towel. *(Collette leaps on Brenda and starts to strangle her.)*

COLLETTE. Did you? Did you? *(Victor pulls her off Brenda.)*

VICTOR. Collette, what are you doing?

BRENDA. She's crazy! Help me!

COLLETTE. "She's crazy! Help me!" Bitch!

VICTOR. What are you doing?

COLLETTE. She locked me in the trailer!

BRENDA. I lost my big scene today!

COLLETTE. Oh, so you're what? Encrazed with grief to

screw me over with your.... What are those? Are those your notes? Lemme see those!

BRADLEY.   Let them go, Victor. This has been coming on for a while.

BRENDA.   These are my ideas! This is America! No Way!

COLLETTE.   Way! *(Collette wrestles the notes from Brenda and reads them.)*

BRENDA.   No! Don't read those! Don't read! Don't read!

COLLETTE.   I am reading.

BRENDA.   Don't!

BRADLEY.   I think she's reading.

COLLETTE.   Oh, you oinking pig!

BRADLEY.   Recent graduates of charm school, no doubt.

COLLETTE.   You couldn't leave me anything, could you?! Have you read these, Victor?

VICTOR.   No, I haven't. *(Collette tears them up.)*

BRENDA.   You can't do that! Those are my ideas! Collette, no!

COLLETTE.   I'm doing you a favor, Brenda. If he saw how greedy you are, he might start to feel about you as I do.

BRENDA.   I hate you.

COLLETTE.   Fine. Just as long as you don't go into that speech about being incested.

BRENDA.   I told you that in confidence!

VICTOR.   She told you about that?

COLLETTE.   She tells everybody about that!

BRENDA.   I do not!

BRADLEY.   She told me. "It's a chain," right?

COLLETTE.   So who's going to save Johnny?

BRENDA.   Me! Make it me!

VICTOR.   Helen.

COLLETTE.   Helen?

BRENDA.   Helen?

COLLETTE.   Who's Helen?

BRENDA.   Helen? Her? You don't even need that character!

BRADLEY.   Helen? My niece plays Helen.

VICTOR.   That's right. And she's a good little actress.

BRADLEY.   Helen. That would be good for my marriage.

COLLETTE. But then it's just a red herring movie.

VICTOR. No, it isn't. Helen is a beautiful character. I just haven't brought her center stage. I can do that in one scene.

BRENDA. But why Helen? Why not me?

COLLETTE. Because you can't act, Brenda! You oughta thank God you're in this movie! You should be selling makeup at Macy's. You walk through your scenes like Bambi with polio!

BRADLEY. JESUS! MY ASS IS ON FIRE! Would anybody mind if I changed my dressing?

COLLETTE. Don't you change that dressing in front of me, you animal!

BRADLEY. Well, I'm not leaving the room! You two harpies might influence Victor to muck up the script.

VICTOR. I can handle myself.

BRADLEY. I believe you, but I'm still not leaving the room.

VICTOR. What's the matter with your ass?

BRENDA. He has a sore on it the size of a jumbo shrimp.

BRADLEY. Not anymore. Now it's the size of a Dungeness Crab!

COLLETTE. Ewww!

VICTOR. I can cut thirteen scenes. Then I'm going home to bury my mother. I'll fix the end later.

BRADLEY. Perfect!

BRENDA. What happened to your mother?

VICTOR. She's dead.

COLLETTE. *(To Brenda.)* Oh, I forgot to tell you. His mother's dead.

BRADLEY. This is gonna salvage George Lee Beech's career, and I believe, literally, it may save my ass.

BRENDA. I'm sorry about your mother.

VICTOR. Thank you.

BRENDA. Please don't cut all my scenes.

COLLETTE. I know why you won't let Brenda save Johnny, but why won't you let me do it? I could do it.

VICTOR. Because, Collette, you're a *character actress!* *(Collette staggers and collapses into a chair.)*

COLLETTE. Ohh! Um! Duh!

BRADLEY. I didn't think you had it in you, Victor! Nice going! Straight, savage, beautiful! Death in the afternoon!

VICTOR. Shut up, Bradley.

BRADLEY. Ladies, I think we may be witnessing the birth of a terrible thing: a movie director.

VICTOR. That's it! That's what you should do! You should fire George and let me take over this picture!

BRADLEY. Don't get ahead of yourself, Victor! There's always another day to stab Caesar. Do you work, go home, and bury your mother.

VICTOR. She's dead, I cried, now my first responsibility is to this picture! You need me! This is a rudderless boat!

BRADLEY. I see your point, but this is George Lee Beech's picture.

VICTOR. I'm not even convinced there is a George Lee Beech. There's some guy you point out and say is George Lee Beech, but how should I know? I don't think anybody's directing this movie and somebody has to!

COLLETTE. Do any of you have a dream that you like, resort to, to escape from this business?

BRADLEY. COME ON, LET ME CHANGE MY DRESSING?!

COLLETTE. NO!

BRENDA. You want me to change it for you?

COLLETTE. Stay away from that! Eww! Skiev!

VICTOR. This movie's about my childhood. My childhood was a mess. This is my chance to straighten it out. Don't deny me that!

BRADLEY. I hear you, but you've got to understand my loyalties.

COLLETTE. Okay, I've come up with a dream

VICTOR. And I guess we're gonna hear it.

COLLETTE. I'm dressed in rags, and I'm missing a few teeth, and I sell apples in the snow. Oh, yeah, and I have my dignity.

BRENDA. How much can you make selling apples?

COLLETTE. Just enough to buy some more apples. (*Brenda and Collette burst into tears.*)

BRADLEY. It's never really about money.

VICTOR.   No, it's not. It's about getting it right. Right, Bradley?

BRADLEY.   Yes, of course. And we will get it right, Victor! You and me and George Lee Beech. That triumvirate. He's given you approvals I wouldn't give to Yahweh. Stayed out of your footpath. You can continue to get that kind of support! You can get this picture right! But hear me when I say, there's beauty to staying in the background. Remember Brutus. He did very well. Till he wanted to direct. And in this case, even if you do wanna direct, do you have to put a name to it? Can't you just do it? The environment is there.

VICTOR.   I see.

BRADLEY.   Just don't put it into words. Put it into action. Quo vadis, Victor, quo vadis?

VICTOR.   All right. It's a deal.

BRADLEY.   And don't worry whether people like you.

VICTOR.   I don't care now. I don't care whether anybody likes me.

BRENDA.   I liked you better before.

COLLETTE.   I never liked you.

BRENDA.   That's true. I never liked him either.

VICTOR.   I knew you never liked me.

BRENDA.   You did?

VICTOR.   Yes.

BRENDA.   Shit!

COLLETTE.   At least we're all talking English now.

VICTOR.   That's right. You're language of choice. *(Bradley opens his arms and states the truth.)*

BRADLEY.   The rain's stopped. We can shoot.

BRENDA.   We're gonna shoot my scene!

VICTOR.   We don't need it. We just need a shot of the two of them, these two, walking away.

BRENDA.   Walking away?

COLLETTE.   Walking away?

BRADLEY.   I don't have to call George if it's a second unit shot. Tell me it's a second unit shot!

VICTOR.   It's a second unit shot. *(Bradley heads for the door.)*

BRADLEY.   I'll get the crew! *(Bradley is gone.)*

BRENDA. Where are we walking?

VICTOR. You don't need to know. *(Brenda starts crying harder.)*

BRENDA. I wanna know where I'm walking!

COLLETTE. I don't. I would be very satisfied to, without any idea of what I'm doing, walk away. Just point me.

VICTOR. You know, I think this is going to be a good movie.

COLLETTE. Hope springs eternal. Among the monkeys.

BRENDA. I really am sorry about your mother. Can we at least walk toward the camera?

VICTOR. We're going to get this together. We're going to have major distribution. This is going to be a Disney Picture!

COLLETTE. Just tell me where to go. Better yet, just draw a line along the ground, and mutely point, and I'll know what you mean.

BRENDA. I swear to God. I do know Bill Goldman's stepson!

COLLETTE. Do I have to be in the shot with her?

BRENDA. I am famous, I am famous, I am famous, I am famous ...

COLLETTE. There she goes. I swear on the experience of my Life, on everything I hold either sacred or profane, I swear to God she's saying Uncle Remus!

THE END

PROPERTY LIST

ACT ONE

Scene 1

Wastepaper basket with picture resumes

On table: magazine with Steven Spielberg on cover
            note paper cube
            pens and pencils in holder
            2 copies of new scene on yellow paper
            tray with: Scotch liquor bottles
                                 glasses
                                 ice bucket with ice cubes
            5 scripts in William Morris Agency covers
            bandages for butt, in decorative holder
            script in black 3-ring binder

Scene 2

On table: full bottle of white wine
            wine glass, full
            stemmed water glass, full
            rocks glass
            dinner plate with half a chicken and sliced carrots
            salt and pepper shakers
            2 candles in glass baskets with netting
            5 fork/knife/napkin set-ups
            1 fork/knife set-up

Off right: rocks cocktail (cranberry juice with ice) (VICTOR)
            call sheet with notes (VICTOR)
            hard-boiled egg (VICTOR)

ACT TWO

Scene 1

Wastepaper basket with used bandage in it

Silk blouse, on chair back

On make-up table: small rotting fruit basket
                                      script, underneath fruit
                                      make-up supplies in tray
                                      clear plastic cup
                                      small water bottle, 8 ounce size, no cap
                                      Visine eye drops

Off left: Purse (COLLETTE) with:
                                    sunglasses
                                    jar of Alka Seltzer

Scene 2

Same as Act One, Scene 1, with:
    Paper with notes, 10 pages, single-spaced (BRENDA)
        (to be torn up each show)
    Money clip with money (BRADLEY)
    Umbrella (VICTOR)
    Delete: magazine on desk

COSTUME PLOT

ACT ONE

SCENE 1
BRENDA: Little black dress
                     Black pumps

BRADLEY: Black-and-white checkered suit
                     White shirt
                     Tie with bears
                     Black shoes

SCENE 2
COLLETTE: White leather dress
                     Gold pumps

VICTOR: Black work pants
                     White T-shirt
                     Black leather jacket
                     Heavy black shoes

ACT TWO

SCENE 1
BRENDA: Green plaid shirtwaist dress (60s)
                     Wig
                     Brown loafers

COLLETTE: Tight black top
                     Leopard jeans (black and gold)
                     Black belt with gold studs
                     Black suede platform booties with buckle

SCENE 2

BRENDA: Same as III but wet

COLLETTE: Same as III but wet

VICTOR: Shiny black raincoat
                 Black dress pants
                 White shirt
                 Black silk knit tie
                 Black dress shoes
                 White umbrella

BRADLEY: White trench coat
                 Khaki pants
                 White button-down shirt
                 Light tie
                 Brown shoes

THE WILD GOOSE

THE WILD GOOSE received its premiere at the Ensemble
Studio Theatre (Curt Dempster, Artistic Director), as part of
the Festival of One-Act Plays, in New York City, on April 29,
1992. It was directed by John Patrick Shanley; the set design
was by Sarah Lambert; the costume design was by Sue Ellen
Roher; the lighting design was by Greg MacPherson; the
sound design was by David Lawson and the stage manager was
Randy Lawson. The cast was as follows:

RENALDO .... Nickolas Turturro
JAMESON ....Robert Clohessy
RAMONA .... Paula DeVicq

THE WILD GOOSE

Two men, Renaldo and Jameson, sit at two tables. Their hair stands on end and there are heavy black circles around their eyes. Renaldo has a pitcher of water, a glass, and a bowl of peanuts. Jameson has a glass and peanuts, but no pitcher. The glasses are currently empty. The two men are incredibly intense and suspicious of each other.

RENALDO.   Do you want water?

JAMESON.   Yes, I do want water.

RENALDO.   Do you want water from me?

JAMESON.   Yes, I do! I want you to get up, come over here, and pour me a glass of water! *(Renaldo gets up and fills Jameson's glass. Then he waits.)*

RENALDO.   Well!

JAMESON.   What?

RENALDO.   Drink it!

JAMESON.   I'm not ready to. *(Renaldo, disgusted, storms back to his table, saying the while.)*

RENALDO.   You asked me to do something for you, I did it, you are in my debt! You should do exactly as I say!

JAMESON.   I don't want to drink it yet.

RENALDO.   When are you going to drink it?

JAMESON.   When I'm thirsty.

RENALDO.   You're not thirsty?

JAMESON.   No.

RENALDO.   Then why did you ask for water?

JAMESON.   Because if there was going to be a problem with you, I wanted to find out before I really needed you. Are you going to have some water? *(Renaldo picks up the pitcher from where he has just placed it, and very messily and savagely drinks the entire contents down. At least what doesn't spill on his clothes and the floor around him, which is a considerable amount. Then he hurls the pitcher away.)*

RENALDO.   Does that answer your question?

JAMESON.   Why did you do that?

RENALDO.   I was thirsty. *(A standoff follows, broken by an outburst from Jameson.)*

JAMESON.   FUCK YOU! FUCK YOU! FUCK YOU! FUCK YOU! *(Another pause, this time violated by Renaldo.)*

RENALDO.   You would say that to me? You would say that to me? After all we've been through? After all that's gone on in the world? After I gave you my water? When you weren't even thirsty? When I was very thirsty? And now I have no water? *(Another standoff, this time broken by Jameson busting out crying.)*

JAMESON.   I'M SORRY! I'M SO SORRY! I DIDN'T UNDERSTAND. I didn't mean it! I didn't know you were thirsty!

RENALDO.   Why didn't you ask?

JAMESON.   I didn't think of it.

RENALDO.   It seems like an obvious question. *(Jameson continues to bawl.)*

JAMESON.   I don't know! You had the pitcher of water and you hadn't even poured yourself any ...

RENALDO.   I was saving it. Because I knew how badly I was going to need it. And I knew how long it was going to be before I could get any again. *(Jameson stops crying.)*

JAMESON.   You mean there's no more water?

RENALDO.   No.

JAMESON.   Anywhere?

RENALDO.   No.

JAMESON.   And you only gave me one glass? That's ugly. *(They consider each other. Then Jameson spots something in the sky.)* Look.

RENALDO.   What?

JAMESON.   Look at that.

RENALDO.   Look at what?

JAMESON.   You don't see it?

RENALDO.   Do you remember Mary? Do you remember Mary Petunias?

JAMESON.   Yes, I remember Mary Petunias.

RENALDO.   Did you ever sleep with her?

JAMESON.   Renaldo?

RENALDO.   Yes?

JAMESON.   Mary Petunias was my wife.

RENALDO.   I know.

JAMESON.   And you're asking me if I slept with her?

RENALDO.   Yes.

JAMESON.   Hey, Buddy, that's a personal question! *(Renaldo jumps suddenly, and grabs his neck.)*

RENALDO.   Ouch!

JAMESON.   What happened?

RENALDO.   I've been stung by a bee!

JAMESON.   Don't worry. The bee will die! Bees die after they sting. That's because they leave their stingers in your neck.

RENALDO.   He did leave his stinger in my neck! I can feel it.

JAMESON.   Do you want me to remove it?

RENALDO.   Would you?

JAMESON.   I don't have pliers.

RENALDO.   You don't have a pair of needlenose pliers?

JAMESON.   No. *(Pulls out a fish.)* All I have is this snapping fish.

RENALDO.   Where'd you get that?

JAMESON.   On your property.

RENALDO.   Fuck you you poacher fuck! Well, come on! *(Jameson gets up, goes to Renaldo, applies the fish to Renaldo's neck.)*

JAMESON.   I think I see the stinger!

RENALDO.   Easy!

JAMESON.   I've got it! *(Jameson pulls a white chunk of stuff out of Renaldo's collar, employing the fish.)* Wait, there's more! *(Pulls out several more white chunks.)*

RENALDO.   Is that it?

JAMESON.   I think that's it.

RENALDO.   Oh, you idiot!

JAMESON.   What?

RENALDO.   That's not a stinger! That's my spine! You have removed my spine!

JAMESON.   Oh, Dearie me!

RENALDO.   You've crippled me!

JAMESON.   Now, come on! Don't overreact.

RENALDO.   You've crippled me with your stupid stupid fish maneuver!

JAMESON.   I can fix it.

RENALDO.   How?

JAMESON.   I can put it back in.

RENALDO.   You don't know how. The greatest surgeon in the world doesn't know how.

JAMESON.   So I don't know how. I don't have to know how. The fish knows how. He took it out and he can put it back in.

RENALDO.   How could a fish know how to perform one of the most complex operations imaginable?

JAMESON.   He didn't at first, but he studied and studied. Now hold still. (*Jameson reverses his procedure, putting the disks back in. He comments meanwhile.*) How are your finances?

RENALDO.   Wretched. Rotten. Grotesque. They stink. I'm broke.

JAMESON.   And why is that?

RENALDO.   I can't make money.

JAMESON.   What about the money you had?

RENALDO.   Oh that! I sold it.

JAMESON.   You sold your money? What did you sell your money for?

RENALDO.   Who else's money could I sell?

JAMESON.   How much did you get for it?

RENALDO.   Oh, I let it go for cheap. I sold it for a song.

JAMESON.   What song?

RENALDO.   An unpopular song. Would you like to hear it?

JAMESON.   No.

RENALDO.   See?

JAMESON.   Maybe I shouldn't give you your back back?

Maybe I should leave you as you are.

RENALDO. Why is that?

JAMESON. Well, isn't it true that the spineless do better financially? *(The two men look at each other and laugh heartily. Renaldo stands and stretches.)*

RENALDO. Good as new! That fish knows what he's doing! *(Jameson takes a bite out of the fish.)*

JAMESON. And he's fresh, too! *(Jameson stows the fish in his pocket. The two men circle each other, wary and a trifle friendly.)*

RENALDO. I fear success!

JAMESON. You have nothing to worry about! *(They each take a peanut, these are the kind with shells, and hold it out like an example for the other to see.)* Will we always be friends?

RENALDO. We're not friends!

JAMESON. Well can we get some kind of continuity out of THAT?

RENALDO. Yeehaii!

JAMESON. I feel very frightened.

RENALDO. How long have you felt frightened?

JAMESON. What a stupid question! You've asked me the wrong question!

RENALDO. Well, what question should I ask?

JAMESON. If I *told* you, it wouldn't be a question! It would be an answer! *(Jameson kisses Renaldo on the cheek. Renaldo hops up and down.)*

RENALDO. You kissed me! You kissed me!

JAMESON. Oh, stop squawking or I won't do it again.

RENALDO. Let us sit together.

JAMESON. Yes, let us sit together. *(They put their chairs side by side and sit down next to each other. They are very happy. They hold their peanuts.)*

RENALDO. Now I am happy!

JAMESON. I am content from my brain to my buttonhole!

RENALDO. If I had the ingredients, I would bake a cake!

JAMESON. All our differences are resolved! Let us eat our nuts!

RENALDO. Look how the jealous squirrels try to look indifferent. *(They shell their peanuts. When each of them has a nut ready to eat, they look at each other. Then they eat. They chew at their peanuts quite a little spell. Then they speak.)*

JAMESON.   Have you ever seen the inside of a peanut?

RENALDO.   Yes! It's like an underground paranoid community without a periscope.   And of course they're right to be paranoid as like as not they will be eaten.

JAMESON.   Have you ever seen the inside of a peanut?

RENALDO.   Yes! It is like a huge monastery of cells inhabited by abstentious contemplative cholesterols.

JAMESON.   Have you ever seen the inside of a peanut?

RENALDO.   Yes! It's like.... Oh. *(The next is done as if everything were fine. Renaldo show no ill effects.)*

JAMESON.   What?

RENALDO.   I'm choking.

JAMESON.   Are you sure?

RENALDO.   Yes.

JAMESON.   Throat locked?

RENALDO.   Yes.

JAMESON.   No air?

RENALDO.   None.

JAMESON.   How long do you think you've got?

RENALDO.   Without the Heimlich?

JAMESON.   Without the Heimlich.

RENALDO.   Not long.

JAMESON.   Do you remember when only movie theatres were air-conditioned? *(Renaldo falls out of his chair, dead.)* I guess he doesn't remember. *(Enter Ramona, with a noose.)*

RAMONA.   Jameson, is that you?

JAMESON.   Ramona! How good that you happened along.

RAMONA.   What's the matter with Renaldo?

JAMESON.   Renaldo is just dead! Just dead! You just missed him! Well Ramona, now you're free!

RAMONA.   I suppose I am. You mean I wasn't?

JAMESON.   Will you marry me?

RAMONA.   Well. I was just going to hang myself.

JAMESON.   With that knot? *(They look at each other and burst out laughing.)* Ah, you can't put a price on friendship!

RAMONA.   Five dollars.

JAMESON. Four!

RAMONA. Two!

JAMESON. Two?!

RAMONA. All right, one!

JAMESON. I can't do it.

RAMONA. Why not?

JAMESON. I don't have money.

RAMONA. Pause.

JAMESON. Did I give you pause?

RAMONA. No. You didn't give me zipper! That's the problem with you, Jameson! You've never given me anything!

JAMESON. I've given you things.

RAMONA. You taco. You've never even given me gas.

JAMESON. Well, you haven't given me ... an answer.

RAMONA. To what?

JAMESON. My proposal. My question.

RAMONA. Hey, don't query me, buster!

JAMESON. I don't want to query you! I want to marry you!

RAMONA. First marry, then query! Do you think I was born in the trunk of a car.

JAMESON. No!

RAMONA. Do you think I was born in a bottle of beer?

JAMESON. No!

RAMONA. Do you think I was born?

JAMESON. Yes.

RAMONA. Well, that's a start.

JAMESON. Pause.

RAMONA. Breath.

JAMESON. *(Sniffs.)* Sniff.

RAMONA. Are you sniffing me?

JAMESON. No. *(Sniffs.)* But I'm sniffing.

RAMONA. That's all well and good, but are you sniffing me?

JAMESON. Not a bit of it. *(Sniffs.)* But I'm sniffing.

RAMONA. My scent is mine.

JAMESON. Tautaulogically true, but explain that to my schnozzol. *(Wiggles his fingers at her.)* Fingers!

RAMONA. *(Reciprocating.)* Fingers back at you!

JAMESON. *(Shaking his foot at her.)* Foot!
RAMONA. *(Reciprocating.)* Foot back at you!
JAMESON. *(A piercing look.)* Eyes!
RAMONA. *(Surrendering.)* The eyes have it.
JAMESON. Holes in us down to the souls in us.
RAMONA. Emotion.
JAMESON. Emotion.
RAMONA. Emotion.
JAMESON. Emotion.
RAMONA. Emotion, emotion.
JAMESON. KEEP SAYING IT AND IT WON'T MEAN A GODDAMN THING!
RAMONA. E.
JAMESON. I'm warning you.
RAMONA. Mo.
JAMESON. Yeah.
RAMONA. Shun.
JAMESON. You got through to me. You were right there heading for gibberish, but the meaning got through. One more time. Like the pony express. The mail got through. People risked their little lives on little horses riding long distances through hordes of little Indians.
RAMONA. Native Americans.
JAMESON. Don't try to control me. So some guy could get a postcard.
RAMONA. Wish you were here.
JAMESON. I do.
RAMONA. And I wish you were here. *(Pause.)*
JAMESON. Now that was a pause. That was not the word "pause." That was the Ding Han Sich. *(Pause.)*
RAMONA. It was a German pause?
JAMESON. If you like.
RAMONA. You are kind.
JAMESON. Kindness lets us breathe.
RAMONA. Maybe that's so.
JAMESON. When we try too hard, we're alone.
RAMONA. Why's that?
JAMESON. I don't know.

RAMONA. The egoism of it.

JAMESON. Yes. The egoism of the Big Try.

RAMONA. And yet you don't want to be slack.

JAMESON. You know what they say. You can pull a string, but you can't push a string.

RAMONA. The sky is enormous.

JAMESON. Pause.

RAMONA. Pause.

JAMESON. Emotion.

RAMONA. Emotion.

JAMESON. Is love so difficult? Is the truth so difficult? Are words so untrustworthy?

RAMONA. You have a couple of problems. One is you don't know what you're talking about. Another is that you're talking.

JAMESON. I am alone! I am alone! I am alone!

RAMONA. What about me?

JAMESON. You are alone, too!

RAMONA. Then what about us?

JAMESON. What about us?

RAMONA. If you're alone, and I'm alone, then what about us?

JAMESON. We have each other!

RAMONA. No. I mean, then are we alone?

JAMESON. Is there someone else here?

RAMONA. I miss Renaldo!

JAMESON. Well, he doesn't miss you! Look, he's found a new friend! A worm!

RAMONA. Oh, you're horrible! Horrible!

JAMESON. I know. I wouldn't live with myself if I had the money.

RAMONA. I miss Renaldo! I miss his face! I miss his voice! *(Ramona is in tears.)*

JAMESON. This is the moment nobody's been waiting for. I'm in hell, woman! I'm just in fucking hell! When this could be paradise. I know it!

RAMONA. In other words, you're in the theatre!

JAMESON. That's it, woman! I'm in the fucking theatre!

Like down at the bottom of the blackest well, the deepest jail!

RAMONA.　　And if you're in the theatre ...

JAMESON.　　The churches are dead! The schools are burning! And I'm in the theatre!

RAMONA.　　Then I'm in the theatre, too! *(Crying out to the audience.)* Confess! Haven't you just had it with the theatre?! I see it in your faces. Confess!

JAMESON.　　Once the gods abandon a place, they never return! Once the gods abandon a temple, a church, a grotto, they never return to that place. That is the historical truth of unrecordable experience!

RAMONA.　　Have the gods left the theatre?

JAMESON.　　You know, I don't believe they have. *(Renaldo jumps up, scaring the heck out of everybody.)*

RENALDO.　　Haiiyaii!

RAMONA.　　OH MY GOD!

RENALDO.　　Hey! Look! I am not dead now!

JAMESON.　　What do you mean you're not dead now?

RENALDO.　　I am not dead now.

JAMESON.　　Were you dead before?

RENALDO.　　*(Holding something back.)* Yes.

RAMONA.　　Were you dead or weren't you?

RENALDO.　　Yes and no.

JAMESON.　　That's no answer!

RENALDO.　　It's no question!

JAMESON.　　Wait! I can't believe my ears!

RENALDO.　　Neither can I! Haven't you got any cotton swabs?

JAMESON.　　That voice! And no! I can't believe my eyes!

RENALDO.　　And yet they're stuck in your face!

JAMESON.　　Renaldo! Did you say your name is Renaldo?

RENALDO.　　Yes.

JAMESON.　　Can it be? Oh, hounds of happiness, how you bite me!

RAMONA.　　Jameson, what is it?

JAMESON.　　Renaldo, when were you born?

RENALDO.　　A long time ago.

JAMESON.　　My God, what a coincidence! Now tell me, sir,

and do not deceive me I beg you! Where were you born?

RENALDO.   I was born on Earth.

JAMESON.   Oh my God! It is too much! That removes my last doubt! You must be my long lost brother Renaldo!

RENALDO.   Holy jumpin' barkin' hotcakes! You must be my long lost brother Jameson!

RENALDO and JAMESON.   How funny ... and strange!

RAMONA.   You mean you're brothers?

RENALDO.   We're more than brothers!

RAMONA.   You're more than brothers? Then what are you? *(Jameson looks at Renaldo, takes out a revolver and shoots Ramona, who falls dead. He tells his brother.)*

JAMESON.   Stupid question.

RENALDO.   Bury her with chairs! *(They cover her with chairs. Renaldo hums "Swing Low, Sweet Chariot." Jameson speaks over her tenderly.)*

JAMESON.   She won't hang herself now.

RENALDO.   No.

JAMESON.   No burial at a crossroad. We won't have to look for a note.

RENALDO.   No.

JAMESON.   We won't have to go to her mother and say, Mam, yer daughter's stretched her own neck!

RENALDO.   We're free of that obligation.

JAMESON.   You're lucky how you jumped up from being dead.

RENALDO.   Pure luck!

JAMESON.   This could just as easily have been you! Under the chairs.

RENALDO.   What a beautiful expression! She's gone under the chairs.

JAMESON.   And someday we'll follow her.

RENALDO.   Under the chairs.

JAMESON.   Would you stop saying that! *(Spots something in the sky again.)* Look!

RENALDO.   What?

JAMESON.   Look at that.

RENALDO.   Look at what?

JAMESON. You don't see it? You really don't see it?

RENALDO. No.

JAMESON. It's the wild goose.

RENALDO. The wild goose? Really?

JAMESON. You still don't see it?

RENALDO. No. *(Jameson takes out his fish and takes a bite.)*

JAMESON. The wild goose is the symbol of the nameless longing that forbids the human heart from ever resting. To hear its call is to know the bittersweet plight of being a man. *(They stand silent. We hear the call of the wild goose. It calls once, twice. Jameson takes out his pistol and fires without hesitation. We hear the goose make a cockeyed death squawk. A big dead goose falls on stage in front of the men. They regard it. Renaldo is deeply moved. He comes down and announces to the audience.)*

RENALDO. The wild goose ... has gone under the chairs.

JAMESON. His tongue lies askew. His noble cry has been stopped. He is one dead metaphor.

RENALDO. This is too painful!

JAMESON. You're right! And yet ...

RENALDO. We can't let our story end this way!

JAMESON. You're right! And yet ...

RENALDO. Who knows but that the wild goose may yet jump up from being dead!

JAMESON. That's true! I feel it! The gods are on the fence about this.

RENALDO. The gods are on the fence about a lot of things.

JAMESON. That's true! And yet but remember, once the gods abandon a place, they never return! That is the historical truth of unrecordable experience!

RENALDO. So we gotta get on this! *(Ramona jumps up, throwing off the chairs.)*

RAMONA. Haiiyaa! It's true! Everything they've been driving at is true! The goose may yet jump up!

JAMESON. Yes! And the gods that inhabit the theatre may yet be enticed to stay!

RENALDO. Yes! And that is why we want you all to sing along with us!

JAMESON.   Get ready! Don't hang back!

RAMONA.   Please! Please, help us! I know you're gonna know this song. Perhaps there isn't much we can agree on! Perhaps there isn't much we can do together! Maybe our culture, unsupported by religion or philosophy or even tax dollars, has completely collapsed into pieces the size of birds' heads! But perhaps maybe at least, we can get it together enough, we can scrape together enough communal feeling, enough brotherly, sisterly trust to sing "Take Me Out To The Ballgame," and resurrect this holy goose! Please! *(Sings.)* "Take me out to the ballgame ..."

JAMESON.   *(Joining.)* Take me out to the crowd ...

RENALDO.   Buy me some peanuts and crackerjacks ... *(The goose lifts his head in response to the song.)*

RAMONA.   It's working! *(She goes back to singing with her two friends and, let's hope, the audience. The goose is rising now, responding to the energy of the song. The song ends. The goose is aloft.)* YES!

JAMESON.   YES!

RENALDO.   YES! AND THANK YOU!

JAMESON.   THANK YOU!

RAMONA.   THANK YOU! *(Jameson closes his eyes to think, pressing his fingers lightly to his temples to better concentrate. The lights all go away except for one on him. He opens his eyes and observes to the audience.)*

JAMESON.   Who knows what else may yet jump up from being dead? *(A recorded version of the song comes up as the actors take their bows.)*

THE END

PROPERTY LIST

Pitcher of water (RENALDO)
Drinking glasses (JAMESON, RENALDO)
2 bowls of peanuts with shells (JAMESON, RENALDO)
Snapping fish (JAMESON)
White chunks of spine (JAMESON)
Noose (RAMONA)
Revolver (JAMESON)
Goose

SOUND EFFECTS

Call of the wild goose
Goose death squawk

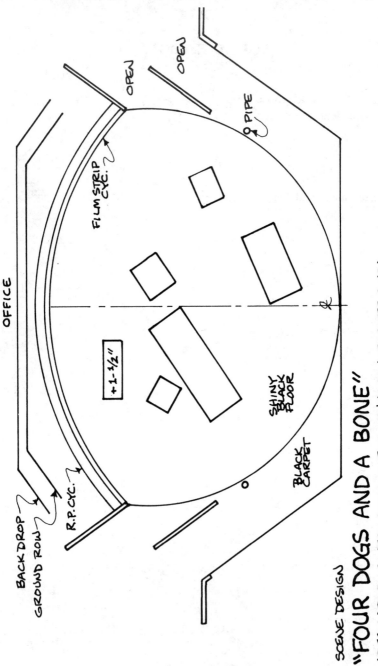

SCENE DESIGN

"FOUR DOGS AND A BONE"

(DESIGNED BY SANTO LOQUASTO FOR MANHATTAN THEATRE CLUB)

NEW PLAYS

★ **AFTER ASHLEY by Gina Gionfriddo.** A teenager is unwillingly thrust into the national spotlight when a family tragedy becomes talk-show fodder. "A work that virtually any audience would find accessible." *—NY Times.* "Deft characterization and caustic humor." *—NY Sun.* "A smart satirical drama." *—Variety.* [4M, 2W] ISBN: 978-0-8222-2099-2

★ **THE RUBY SUNRISE by Rinne Groff.** Twenty-five years after Ruby struggles to realize her dream of inventing the first television, her daughter faces similar battles of faith as she works to get Ruby's story told on network TV. "Measured and intelligent, optimistic yet clear-eyed." *—NY Magazine.* "Maintains an exciting sense of ingenuity." *—Village Voice.* "Sinuous theatrical flair." *—Broadway.com.* [3M, 4W] ISBN: 978-0-8222-2140-1

★ **MY NAME IS RACHEL CORRIE taken from the writings of Rachel Corrie, edited by Alan Rickman and Katharine Viner.** This solo piece tells the story of Rachel Corrie who was killed in Gaza by an Israeli bulldozer set to demolish a Palestinian home. "Heartbreaking urgency. An invigoratingly detailed portrait of a passionate idealist." *—NY Times.* "Deeply authentically human." *—USA Today.* "A stunning dramatization." *—CurtainUp.* [1W] ISBN: 978-0-8222-2222-4

★ **ALMOST, MAINE by John Cariani.** This charming midwinter night's dream of a play turns romantic clichés on their ear as it chronicles the painfully hilarious amorous adventures (and misadventures) of residents of a remote northern town that doesn't quite exist. "A whimsical approach to the joys and perils of romance." *—NY Times.* "Sweet, poignant and witty." *—NY Daily News.* "Aims for the heart by way of the funny bone." *—Star-Ledger.* [2M, 2W] ISBN: 978-0-8222-2156-2

★ **Mitch Albom's TUESDAYS WITH MORRIE by Jeffrey Hatcher and Mitch Albom, based on the book by Mitch Albom.** The true story of Brandeis University professor Morrie Schwartz and his relationship with his student Mitch Albom. "A touching, life-affirming, deeply emotional drama." *—NY Daily News.* "You'll laugh. You'll cry." *—Variety.* "Moving and powerful." *—NY Post.* [2M] ISBN: 978-0-8222-2188-3

★ **DOG SEES GOD: CONFESSIONS OF A TEENAGE BLOCKHEAD by Bert V. Royal.** An abused pianist and a pyromaniac ex-girlfriend contribute to the teen-angst of America's most hapless kid. "A welcome antidote to the notion that the *Peanuts* gang provides merely American cuteness." *—NY Times.* "Hysterically funny." *—NY Post.* "The *Peanuts* kids have finally come out of their shells." *—Time Out.* [4M, 4W] ISBN: 978-0-8222-2152-4

DRAMATISTS PLAY SERVICE, INC.
440 Park Avenue South, New York, NY 10016 212-683-8960 Fax 212-213-1539
postmaster@dramatists.com www.dramatists.com

NEW PLAYS

★ **RABBIT HOLE by David Lindsay-Abaire.** Winner of the 2007 Pulitzer Prize. Becca and Howie Corbett have everything a couple could want until a life-shattering accident turns their world upside down. "An intensely emotional examination of grief, laced with wit." *–Variety.* "A transcendent and deeply affecting new play." *–Entertainment Weekly.* "Painstakingly beautiful." *–BackStage.* [2M, 3W] ISBN: 978-0-8222-2154-8

★ **DOUBT, A Parable by John Patrick Shanley.** Winner of the 2005 Pulitzer Prize and Tony Award. Sister Aloysius, a Bronx school principal, takes matters into her own hands when she suspects the young Father Flynn of improper relations with one of the male students. "All the elements come invigoratingly together like clockwork." *–Variety.* "Passionate, exquisite, important, engrossing." *–NY Newsday.* [1M, 3W] ISBN: 978-0-8222-2219-4

★ **THE PILLOWMAN by Martin McDonagh.** In an unnamed totalitarian state, an author of horrific children's stories discovers that someone has been making his stories come true. "A blindingly bright black comedy." *–NY Times.* "McDonagh's least forgiving, bravest play." *–Variety.* "Thoroughly startling and genuinely intimidating." *–Chicago Tribune.* [4M, 5 bit parts (2M, 1W, 1 boy, 1 girl)] ISBN: 978-0-8222-2100-5

★ **GREY GARDENS book by Doug Wright, music by Scott Frankel, lyrics by Michael Korie.** The hilarious and heartbreaking story of Big Edie and Little Edie Bouvier Beale, the eccentric aunt and cousin of Jacqueline Kennedy Onassis, once bright names on the social register who became East Hampton's most notorious recluses. "An experience no passionate theatergoer should miss." *–NY Times.* "A unique and unmissable musical." *–Rolling Stone.* [4M, 3W, 2 girls] ISBN: 978-0-8222-2181-4

★ **THE LITTLE DOG LAUGHED by Douglas Carter Beane.** Mitchell Green could make it big as the hot new leading man in Hollywood if Diane, his agent, could just keep him in the closet. "Devastatingly funny." *–NY Times.* "An out-and-out delight." *–NY Daily News.* "Full of wit and wisdom." *–NY Post.* [2M, 2W] ISBN: 978-0-8222-2226-2

★ **SHINING CITY by Conor McPherson.** A guilt-ridden man reaches out to a therapist after seeing the ghost of his recently deceased wife. "Haunting, inspired and glorious." *–NY Times.* "Simply breathtaking and astonishing." *–Time Out.* "A thoughtful, artful, absorbing new drama." *–Star-Ledger.* [3M, 1W] ISBN: 978-0-8222-2187-6

DRAMATISTS PLAY SERVICE, INC.
440 Park Avenue South, New York, NY 10016 212-683-8960 Fax 212-213-1539
postmaster@dramatists.com www.dramatists.com